Instant OpenCV for iOS

Learn how to build real-time computer vision applications
for the iOS platform using the OpenCV library

Kirill Kornyakov

Alexander Shishkov

BIRMINGHAM - MUMBAI

Instant OpenCV for iOS

First published: August 2013

Production Reference: 1230813

Published by Packt Publishing Ltd.
Livery Place
35 Livery Street
Birmingham B3 2PB, UK.

ISBN 978-1-78216-384-8

www.packtpub.com

Credits

Authors

Kirill Kornyakov

Alexander Shishkov

Reviewers

Emmanuel d'Angelo

Jean-David Gadina

Acquisition Editor

Usha Iyer

Commissioning Editor

Subho Gupta

Technical Editor

Dennis John

Project Coordinator

Akash Poojary

Proofreader

Clyde Jenkins

Production Coordinator

Prachali Bhiwandkar

Cover Work

Prachali Bhiwandkar

Cover Image

Conidon Miranda

About the Authors

Kirill Kornyakov has been a member of core OpenCV development team for the last 4 years. He works at Itseez (Nizhny Novgorod, Russia), where he leads the development of an OpenCV library for the Android operating system, with a focus on performance optimization for the NVIDIA Tegra platform. He also works on implementation of real-time computer vision algorithms, mainly computational photography applications. Kirill has B.Sc. and M.Sc. degrees from Nizhny Novgorod State University, Russia.

> To Nina and Brusnichka, whose warmth gives me strength.

Alexander Shishkov has been working in the field of computer vision for the last five years. He works at Itseez (Nizhny Novgorod, Russia), where he has developed technologies such as video-based people counting systems, object detection, and image retrieval systems. He also created continuous integration system and websites (http://opencv.org) for OpenCV. Alexander has B.Sc. and M.Sc. degrees from Nizhny Novgorod State University, Russia.

> I want to thank my family who supported and encouraged me in spite of all the time I was away from them.

About the Reviewers

Emmanuel d'Angelo is an image processing enthusiast who has turned his hobby into a job. After working as a technical consultant on various projects ranging from real-time image stabilization to large-scale image database analysis, he is now in charge of developing Digital Signal Processing (DSP) applications on low-power consumer devices. You can find more insight about his research and image processing-related information on his blog at `http://www.computersdontsee.net/`.

Emmanuel holds a Ph.D. degree from the Swiss Federal Institute of Technology (EPFL, Switzerland) and a Master's degree in Remote Sensing from ISAE (Toulouse, France).

Jean-David Gadina is a software developer from Lausanne, Switzerland.

He has a lot of experience in languages, such as C, Objective-C, C++, and x86 assembly, and develops software for desktop (Mac/Windows) and mobile devices (iOS).

Jean-David currently works for DigiDNA (`www.digidna.net`), a Swiss and Australian software company specializing in data management and transfer between Apple mobile the devices and computers. DigiDNA produces DiskAid, an iPhone file transfer software for the PC and Mac, as well as FileApp, an iPhone filesystem and document viewer.

In his spare time, Jean-David enjoys working on the development of an operating system, as well as on other open source tools and software libraries.

You can check out Jean-David's blog at `www.noxeos.com`, or follow him on Twitter (`@macmade`).

www.PacktPub.com

Support files, eBooks, discount offers and more

You might want to visit www.packtpub.com for support files and downloads related to your book.

Did you know that Packt offers eBook versions of every book published, with PDF and ePub files available? You can upgrade to the eBook version at www.packtpub.com and as a print book customer, you are entitled to a discount on the eBook copy. Get in touch with us at service@packtpub.com for more details.

At www.packtpub.com, you can also read a collection of free technical articles, sign up for a range of free newsletters and receive exclusive discounts and offers on Packt books and eBooks.

http://PacktLib.packtpub.com

Do you need instant solutions to your IT questions? PacktLib is Packt's online digital book library. Here, you can access, read and search across Packt's entire library of books.

Why Subscribe?

- ▸ Fully searchable across every book published by Packt
- ▸ Copy and paste, print and bookmark content
- ▸ On demand and accessible via web browser

Free Access for Packt account holders

If you have an account with Packt at www.packtpub.com, you can use this to access PacktLib today and view nine entirely free books. Simply use your login credentials for immediate access.

Table of Contents

Preface 1

Instant OpenCV for iOS 5

  Getting started with iOS (Simple) 5

  Displaying an image from resources (Simple) 10

  Linking OpenCV to an iOS project (Simple) 15

  Detecting faces with Cascade Classifier (Intermediate) 21

  Printing a postcard (Intermediate) 24

  Working with images in Gallery (Intermediate) 30

  Applying a retro effect (Intermediate) 37

  Taking photos from camera (Intermediate) 41

  Creating a static library (Intermediate) 46

  Capturing a video from camera (Simple) 50

  Control advanced camera settings (Advanced) 55

  Applying effects to live video (Intermediate) 60

  Saving video from camera (Simple) 63

  Optimizing performance with ARM NEON (Advanced) 65

  Detecting facial features (Advanced) 72

  Using the Accelerate framework (Advanced) 77

  Building OpenCV for iOS from sources (Advanced) 81

Preface

Instant OpenCV for iOS is a practical guide, showing every important step for building a computer vision application for the iOS platform. It will help you to port your OpenCV code, profile and optimize it, and then wrap into a GUI application. This book helps you to learn how to build a simple, but powerful computer vision application for the iOS devices from scratch. Throughout the book, you'll learn details that will help you to become a professional at iOS development using OpenCV. As usual, you begin with the simple "Hello World" application, but finally you will be able to create complex image processing applications with supreme efficiency.

Each recipe is accompanied with a sample project, helping you to focus on a particular aspect of the technology.

What this book covers

- *Getting started with iOS (Simple)*, helps you to set up your development environment and run your first "Hello World" iOS application.

- *Displaying an image from resources (Simple)*, introduces you to basic GUI concepts on iOS, and covers loading of an image from resources and displaying it on the screen.

- *Linking OpenCV to an iOS project (Simple)*, explains how to link OpenCV library and call any function from it.

- *Detecting faces with Cascade Classifier (Intermediate)*, shows how to detect faces using OpenCV.

- *Printing a postcard (Intermediate)*, demonstrates how a simple photo effect can be implemented.

- *Working with images in Gallery (Intermediate)*, explains how to load and save images from/to Gallery.

- *Applying a retro effect (Intermediate)*, demonstrates another interesting photo effect that makes photos look old.

- *Taking photos from camera (Intermediate)*, shows how to capture static images with camera.

- ▶ *Creating a static library (Intermediate)*, explains how to create a static library project in Xcode.

- ▶ *Capturing a video from camera (Simple)*, shows how to capture a video stream from camera.

- ▶ *Control advanced camera settings (Advanced)*, explains how to control advanced camera settings, such as exposure, focus, and white balance.

- ▶ *Applying effects to live video (Intermediate)*, shows how to process captured video frames on the fly.

- ▶ *Saving video from camera (Simple)*, explains how to save video stream to the device with hardware encoding.

- ▶ *Optimizing the performance with ARM NEON (Advanced)*, explains how to use SIMD instructions to vectorize your code and improve the performance.

- ▶ *Detecting facial features (Advanced)*, presents a simple facial feature detection demo.

- ▶ *Using the Accelerate framework (Advanced)*, explains how to link the framework, and how to use it for performance optimization.

- ▶ *Building OpenCV for iOS from sources (Advanced)*, explains where to get and how to build the latest OpenCV sources.

What you need for this book

In order to be able to build and run sample projects from this book, you will need a Mac OS X computer, as it is the only supported way to develop for iOS platform. You should also have a device with iOS 6.0 or higher, because Simulator doesn't support camera, and some projects will not work on it.

Finally, you need the latest version of Xcode, so you can modify, build, and execute examples from this book.

Who this book is for

This book is intended for OpenCV developers who are interested in porting their applications to the iOS platform. You need to have some basic experience with OpenCV and computer vision, but can be a beginner in Objective-C or other iOS tools. The book could be also helpful for those who are familiar with iOS and want to add some image processing or computer vision functionality to their projects.

Conventions

In this book, you will find a number of styles of text that distinguish between different kinds of information. Here are some examples of these styles, and an explanation of their meaning.

Code words in text are shown as follows: "The `NSLog` function, which we added first, is intended for logging simple text messages, similar to the `printf` function in the C language."

A block of code is set as follows:

```
-  (void) viewDidLoad
{
    [super viewDidLoad];

    // Read the image
    image = [UIImage imageNamed:@"lena.png"];
    if (image != nil)
        imageView.image = image;
}
```

Any command-line input or output is written as follows:

```
$ cd /
$ sudo ln -s /Applications/Xcode.app/Contents/Developer Developer
```

New terms and **important words** are shown in bold. Words that you see on the screen, in menus or dialog boxes for example, appear in the text like this: "As we know the resolution of the camera only after session starts, we should create a filter object when the **StartCapture** button is clicked".

 Warnings or important notes appear in a box like this.

 Tips and tricks appear like this.

Reader feedback

Feedback from our readers is always welcome. Let us know what you think about this book—what you liked or may have disliked. Reader feedback is important for us to develop titles that you really get the most out of.

To send us general feedback, simply send an e-mail to `feedback@packtpub.com`, and mention the book title via the subject of your message.

If there is a topic that you have expertise in and you are interested in either writing or contributing to a book, see our author guide on `www.packtpub.com/authors`.

Customer support

Now that you are the proud owner of a Packt book, we have a number of things to help you to get the most from your purchase.

Downloading the example code

You can download the example code files for all Packt books you have purchased from your account at http://www.packtpub.com. If you purchased this book elsewhere, you can visit http://www.packtpub.com/support and register to have the files e-mailed directly to you.

Errata

Although we have taken every care to ensure the accuracy of our content, mistakes do happen. If you find a mistake in one of our books—maybe a mistake in the text or the code—we would be grateful if you would report this to us. By doing so, you can save other readers from frustration and help us improve subsequent versions of this book. If you find any errata, please report them by visiting http://www.packtpub.com/submit-errata, selecting your book, clicking on the **errata submission form** link, and entering the details of your errata. Once your errata are verified, your submission will be accepted and the errata will be uploaded on our website, or added to any list of existing errata, under the Errata section of that title. Any existing errata can be viewed by selecting your title from http://www.packtpub.com/support.

Piracy

Piracy of copyright material on the Internet is an ongoing problem across all media. At Packt, we take the protection of our copyright and licenses very seriously. If you come across any illegal copies of our works, in any form, on the Internet, please provide us with the location address or website name immediately so that we can pursue a remedy.

Please contact us at copyright@packtpub.com with a link to the suspected pirated material.

We appreciate your help in protecting our authors, and our ability to bring you valuable content.

Questions

You can contact us at questions@packtpub.com if you are having a problem with any aspect of the book, and we will do our best to address it.

Instant OpenCV for iOS

Instant OpenCV for iOS is a practical guide, showing every important step for building a computer vision application for the iOS platform. It will help you port your OpenCV code, profile and optimize it, and then wrap into a GUI application. Each recipe is accompanied with a sample project, helping you focus on a particular aspect of the technology.

Getting started with iOS (Simple)

In this recipe, we'll provide all the necessary steps to set up your environment and run a "Hello World" application on a device. Development for the iOS platform may seem to be difficult in the beginning, because the list of prerequisites is somewhat large. We'll provide important links for those who are not familiar with Mac/iOS development, Objective-C, and Xcode. If you're already familiar with the iOS development, you can skip this recipe.

Getting ready

Apple has established a very rich and sound ecosystem for developers, where each component is tightly integrated with others. Once you're familiar with its basic rules and principles, you'll be able to switch between different types of projects easily. But it may take some time to familiarize yourself with the tools and frameworks. And the very first prerequisite for iOS development is a Mac OS X workstation or laptop, and you cannot use other operating systems. It is also highly recommended to use the latest available version of the OS and tools, as some new features are not backported to older versions. Currently, the latest version is the Mac OS X 10.8, also known as *Mountain Lion*.

 Unfortunately, you can't move forward without a Mac, but if you're new to this platform, it could become a very rewarding experience. Proficiency with multiple platforms is beneficial for your professional skills.

Secondly, to run some examples from this book, you will definitely need an iOS device, because iOS Simulator lacks camera support. You should also know that Simulator executes x86 native code, while real iOS devices are running on ARM. This difference will not allow you to understand the actual performance of your application, which is usually important. You can use a simple device such as iPod Touch, which is quite cheap and may be useful not only for development! But of course, we recommend you to find one of the latest iOS devices; currently these are iPhone 5 and iPad 4. The iOS version should be 6.0 or higher.

> Actually, you can use Simulator for experimenting with many examples in this book. It is also a good chance to test your application on a tablet if you only have a phone, or vise versa. But please note that samples that need camera will not work. Every time you need a real device, we will mention that in the beginning of the recipe.

When you have all the hardware, you'll need to install Xcode—the cornerstone of all Mac-centric development. You will need Version 4.6.3 or higher. We recommend installing it together with the command-line tools, so you'll have access to compiler and some other tools from the Terminal.

We're almost ready to start development, and you can actually proceed to the following *How to do it...* section if you're going to use Simulator. But if you're going to use a real device now or later, there is one more step. In order to run your application on a real device, you have to become a registered Apple developer (which is free), and you will also need to subscribe for the **iOS Developer Program**, which will cost you $99 per year. This may look too high for the opportunity to play with your little applications, but this is how Apple verifies that you're serious, and that you will do your best to create a decent app. Also, it gives you access to all beta software from Apple, related to iOS, which is very important from a developer's perspective. Registration procedure is described at `https://developer.apple.com/register/index.action`, and the page about the "iOS Developer Program" is at `https://developer.apple.com/programs/ios/`. Finally, you need to register your device according to this instruction found at `http://bit.ly/3848_DeviceProvisioning`.

Source code for this recipe is available in the `Recipe01_HelloWorld` folder in the code bundle that accompanies this book.

> **Downloading the example code**
>
> You can download the example code files for all Packt books you have purchased from your account at `http://www.packtpub.com`. If you purchased this book elsewhere, you can visit `http://www.packtpub.com/support` and register to have the files e-mailed directly to you.

How to do it...

So, now we're ready to create our first "Hello World" application, and it's going to be in Objective-C. The following are the steps required to achieve our goal:

1. Connect your device to the host computer.

2. Open Xcode and create a new project.

3. Modify the code, so that the "Hello World" text will appear.

4. Run the application.

Let's implement the described steps:

1. We'll start by connecting your device to the computer (you can skip this step in case you're using Simulator). This is done using the USB cable, and it not only allows you to charge your device, but also provides some control over it. There are some applications available that allow you to copy files from/to a connected device (for example, iFunBox), but we'll not need it, because we'll be using Xcode to communicate with the device.

2. Next, we'll launch Xcode. When started, Xcode will show your menu with several options, and you should choose the **Create a new Xcode project** option. Then you need to choose **Single View Application** template by navigating to **iOS | Application**. In the dialog box that appears, you have to specify values for **Product Name**, **Organization Name** (you can use your name), and **Company Identifier**. The following screenshot shows the window with options for creating a new project:

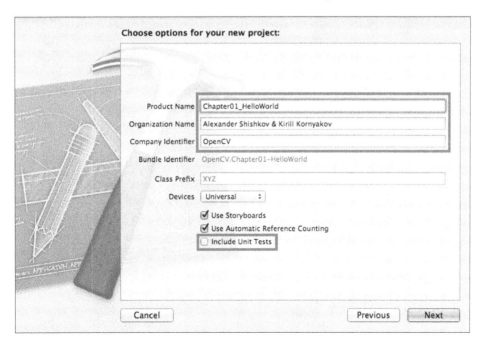

3. We also recommend you uncheck the **Include Unit Tests** checkbox, because we don't need them for now. Then click on **Next**, choose a folder for you project, click on **Create**, and you're done!

4. Now it's time to add some handcrafted code to the auto-generated project. You can see that the Xcode window is divided into several "areas". The following screenshot is taken from the official Xcode User Guide, explaining the layout (`http://bit.ly/3848_Xcode`):

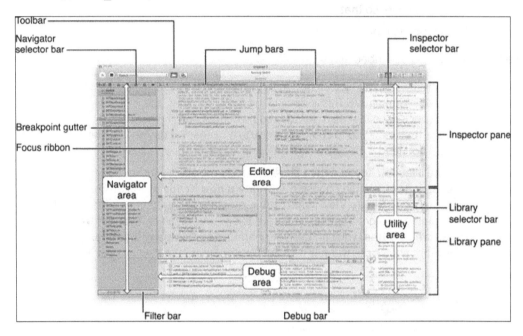

5. Open the `ViewController.m` file, which can be found in the **Project Navigator Area** on the left-hand side. We're going to add a simple logging to the console, and an alert window. In order to do that, please edit the `viewDidLoad` method, so it looks like the following code:

```
- (void)viewDidLoad
{
    [super viewDidLoad];

    // Console output
    NSLog(@"Hello, World!");

    // Alert window
    UIAlertView *alert = [UIAlertView alloc];
    alert = [alert initWithTitle:@"Hey there!"
                         message:@"Welcome to OpenCV on iOS \
                                  development community"
```

```
                         delegate:nil
                 cancelButtonTitle:@"Continue"
                 otherButtonTitles:nil];

        [alert show];
    }
```

6. Then open the **Debug Area** in the Xcode navigating to **View | Debug Area | Show Debug Area**. Now click on the **Run** button located in the top-left corner of the Xcode window, and check that you can see both the alert window on the device's screen and the log message in the **Debug Area**. That's it; you have your first application running!

How it works...

The NSLog function, which we added first, is intended for logging simple text messages, similar to the printf function in the C language. You can also see that our string was preceded with the @ character, which is used for implicit conversion to the NSString object. Just like printf, NSLog allows you to print values of multiple variables with proper formatting, so this function is quite helpful during debugging and profiling of your application.

 While the NSLog function is useful for logging, you should not keep these logs in the production code because like any other IO procedure, it has its cost, which may negatively affect the performance. So, you should use conditional compilation or something else to remove all debug logs from the release code.

The next code block shows how one can create a simple message window with some notification. We are not going to use UIAlertView in later recipes, but this is a good occasion to get familiar with creating objects and calling their methods in Objective-C. The first line shows how a new object may be created. Here, the alloc method is called that was inherited by UIAlertView from its parent NSObject class. Next, we're calling the initWithTitle method, passing necessary arguments to it. This method returns a newly initialized alert window. Finally, we call the show method to display the window with our message.

Please note that we've reformatted the code for readability, and we've even created one surplus temporary object. It was possible to call the initWithTitle method of a newly allocated object, so in most cases, you will likely meet the initialization code as shown in the following code snippet.

```
UIAlertView * alert = [[UIAlertView alloc] initWithTitle:@"Hey there!"
message:@"Welcome to OpenCV on iOS development community" delegate:nil
cancelButtonTitle:@"Continue" otherButtonTitles:nil];
```

There's more...

That's all for this recipe, but if you feel that you need some more introductory information on iOS development in general, we'll provide you with some pointers. Later, we will focus mostly on OpenCV-related aspects of programming, so if you want to better understand Apple's tools and frameworks, you should spend some time studying other resources.

Xcode

We encourage you to "sharpen your saw" and read more about Xcode. Refer to the official documentation at `https://developer.apple.com/xcode/`. For example, you can create several Simulators to test your application on different types of devices. Navigate to **Xcode | Preferences**, and then go to the **Downloads | Components** to see the available options. Many useful tips on Xcode and sample code examples are available in the iOS Developer Library at `http://developer.apple.com/library/ios/navigation/`.

Objective-C

One of the important things you should know about Objective-C is that it is a strict superset of C, and you can mix it with C. Because OpenCV is written in C++, we have to use Objective-C++, which allows to use a combination of C++ and Objective-C syntax and also allows you to reuse your C++ code or libraries (as we do with OpenCV). Nonetheless, Objective-C is the main language for iOS, so you should get familiar with it in order to use the available libraries and frameworks effectively.

Displaying an image from resources (Simple)

Every application may keep some images in its resources, such as textures or icons. In this recipe, we'll study how one can add an image to resources, load it into the `UIImage` object, and then display it on the screen. We will use the `UIImageView` component for that purpose, and get familiar with the important **Model-View-Controller** (**MVC**) design pattern.

Getting ready

Source code for this recipe is available in the `Recipe02_DisplayingImage` folder in the code bundle that accompanies this book. You can also take your own image with the preferred 320 x 480 resolution. Or, you can use the provided `lena.png` image, based on the famous picture among computer vision engineers (`http://lenna.org`). You can use iOS Simulator to work on this recipe.

How to do it...

The following are the steps required to display an image:

1. Add an image to the project's resources.

2. Add `UIImageView` component to the View.

3. Add image loading code.

4. Display an image on the screen.

Let's implement the described steps:

1. For this example, you can use the Xcode project created in the previous recipe. We'll start by adding an image to the project. For that purpose, you should use the **Add files to ...** context menu from the **Project Navigator Area**. In the opened window, you should select the image and click on the **Add** button. The filename should appear in the **Supporting Files** group of the **Project Navigator Area**.

2. Next, we'll add the `UIImageView` component to our View. For that purpose, you have to open the storyboard file corresponding to your device in the **Project Navigator Area**. Initially it looks like a blank panel. You should find the **Image View** component in the **Objects** list located in the bottom-right corner of the Xcode window and drag it to the View. In the following screenshot, you can see the **Objects** list in storyboard editor:

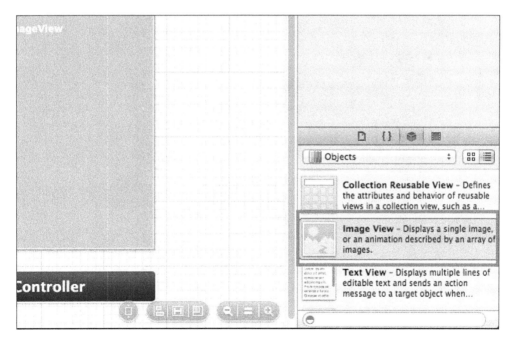

3. We now have the View for displaying images, but it doesn't have any code-behind. In order to add some logic, we should first add a special variable to our Controller class. In order to do that, change the interface of the `ViewController` class in the `ViewController.h` file as follows:

```
@interface ViewController : UIViewController {
    UIImage* image;
}
@property (nonatomic, weak) IBOutlet UIImageView* imageView;
@end
```

4. Then we should connect the newly created property and the visual component on our View. Open storyboard again and turn on the **Assistant Editor** mode by navigating to **View | Assistant Editor | Show Assistant Editor**. After that, the main Xcode window will be split into two parts. On one side you can find the `ViewController.h` file, and the storyboard will be shown on the other side. Connect the `imageView` property with the `UIImageView` component, as shown in the following screenshot:

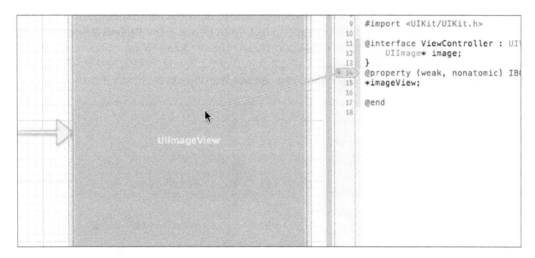

5. Now it's time to add some code to the Controller's implementation file. If you use your own image, please change the filename accordingly, as shown in the following code snippet:

```
#import "ViewController.h"

@interface ViewController ()
@end

@implementation ViewController
@synthesize imageView;

- (void)viewDidLoad
```

```
{
    [super viewDidLoad];

    // Read the image
    image = [UIImage imageNamed:@"lena.png"];
    if (image != nil)
        imageView.image = image; // Displaying the image
}
```

6. That's all; you can now run your application by clicking on the **Run** button.

How it works...

In this recipe we have implemented our first GUI on iOS. We'll now discuss some basic concepts related to GUI development. The most important idea is using Model-View-Controller design pattern, which separates visual representation, user interaction logic, and the core logic of the application. There are three parts in this pattern:

1. **Model**: This contains business logic, such as data and algorithms for data processing. It does not know how this information should be presented to the user.

2. **View**: This is responsible for visualization. It can be imagined as some GUI form with visual components on it (for example, buttons, labels, and so on).

3. **Controller**: This provides communication between the user and the system core. It monitors the user's input and uses Model and a View to implement the necessary response.

Usually, applications have several Views with some rules to switch between them. Also, simple programs usually contain only two parts of the pattern: View and Controller, because logic is very simple, and developers do not create a separate entity for the Model.

A View is created as a storyboard element. The file with the *.storyboard extension allows you to describe an interface of your application with all internal elements. Xcode contains a special graphical tool to add visual controls and change their parameters. So, all that you need is to fill your View with the needed GUI components using drag-and-drop.

 All our examples are based on the storyboards mechanism that was introduced in iOS 5. It is a great intuitive way to describe all interactions between visual components of your application. If you want to support devices with the iOS version older than 5, you should use .xib files to describe the application interface.

When you create a new project, Xcode adds two storyboards for different device families (`MainStoryboard_iPhone.storyboard` and `MainStoryboard_iPad.storyboard`). Of course, you can use a single storyboard for all devices. For this purpose, you should change value of the **Main Storyboard** property in **Deployment Settings** of the project. But tablets and smartphones differ much in screen resolutions, so it is highly recommended to create separate Views with different layouts for both families.

For each View, you should normally have a Controller. For every new project, Xcode creates a `ViewController` class by default (`ViewController.h` and `ViewController.m` files). In our example, we first add the `IBOutlet` property to the interface declaration of our View. `IBOutlet` is a special macro to denote a variable that can be attached to some visual component on the View. `IBOutlet` resolves to nothing, but it makes clear to Xcode that such variables can be linked with UI elements.

In our implementation, we use the `@property` keyword. By default, if we add some variable to the Controller's interface (as well as to any other interface), it will be private, so we can't access it out of the class. If we want to do it, we can use the `@property` keyword. It is somewhat added as an instance variable, but it requires you to implement getter and setter methods. In our example, we do it by calling another special `@synthesize` keyword. It automatically generates getter and setter methods for your variable.

In this recipe, we add some code to the `viewDidLoad` method of the `ViewController` class. This method is a good place to show our image, because it is called after the `ViewController` has been loaded. You may have noticed that this method already had the following line:

```
[super viewDidLoad];
```

It is just a call of the `viewDidLoad` method implemented in the superclass. Here we use `UIImage` object to load an image from the file. `UIImage` is a high-level class to store and display image data. It is similar to `cv::Mat` class as an image container, but can't be used for mathematical computations.

To display the image on the View, we just need to assign the variable with the loaded image to the `imageView.image` property.

There's more...

You have the possibility to implement getters and setters manually:

```
- (UIImageView*) imageView
{
    return imageView1;
}

- (void) setImageView: (UIImageView*) newImageView
```

```
{
  if (newImageView != imageView1)
  {
   imageView1 = newImageView;
  }
}
```

Cocoa design patterns

In this recipe, we get familiar with one of the most important Cocoa design patterns—Model-View-Controller. But there are other important patterns that you should know to design your applications properly. We encourage you to study the Cocoa Fundamentals Guide (`http://bit.ly/3848_CocoaFundamentalsGuide`) and the Cocoa Design Patterns article in particular (`http://bit.ly/3848_CocoaDesignPatterns`).

Linking OpenCV to an iOS project (Simple)

For now, we have some basic framework for testing image processing and computer vision algorithms. Now it's time to add OpenCV to your project and add your first call to the library. You will learn how to convert `UIImage` to `cv::Mat`, and make a call to the C++ library using Objective-C code.

Getting ready

First you should download the OpenCV framework for iOS from the official website at `http://opencv.org`. In this book, we will use Version 2.4.6. You can use the iOS Simulator to work on this recipe. Source code for this recipe can be found in the `Recipe03_LinkingOpenCV` folder in the code bundle that accompanies this book.

How to do it...

The following are the main steps to accomplish the task:

1. Add the OpenCV framework to your project.
2. Convert image to the OpenCV format.
3. Process image with a simple OpenCV call.
4. Convert image back.
5. Display image as before.

Let's implement the described steps:

1. We continue modifying the previous project, so that you can use it; otherwise create a new project with `UIImageView`. We'll start by adding the OpenCV framework to the Xcode project. There are two ways to do it.

    You can add the framework as a resource as described in previous recipe. This is a straightforward approach. Alternatively, the framework can be added through project properties by navigating to **Project | Build Phases | Link Binary With Libraries**. To open project properties you should click to the project name in the **Project Navigator** area.

2. Next, we'll include OpenCV header files to our project. In order to do so, we will modify the `Recipe03_LinkingOpenCV-Prefix.pch` precompiled header. To avoid conflicts, we will add the following code to the very beginning of the file, above all other imports:

    ```
    #ifdef __cplusplus
    #import <opencv2/opencv.hpp>
    #endif
    ```

    This is needed, because OpenCV redefines some names, for example, `min/max` functions.

3. Set the value of **Compile Sources As** property as **Objective-C++**. The property is available in the project settings and can be accessed by navigating to **Project | Build Settings | Apple LLVM compiler 4.1 - Language**.

4. To convert the images from `UIImage` to `cv::Mat`, you can use the following functions:

    ```
    UIImage* MatToUIImage(const cv::Mat& image)
    {
        NSData *data = [NSData dataWithBytes:image.data length:image.
    elemSize()*image.total()];

        CGColorSpaceRef colorSpace;

        if (image.elemSize() == 1) {
            colorSpace = CGColorSpaceCreateDeviceGray();
        } else {
            colorSpace = CGColorSpaceCreateDeviceRGB();
        }

        CGDataProviderRef provider = CGDataProviderCreateWithCFData((__
    bridge CFDataRef)data);

        // Creating CGImage from cv::Mat
        CGImageRef imageRef = CGImageCreate(image.cols,    //width
    ```

```
                                    image.rows,    //height
                                    8,             //bits per
component
                                    8*image.elemSize(),//bits
per pixel
                                    image.step.p[0],   //
bytesPerRow
                                    colorSpace,    //colorspace
                  kCGImageAlphaNone|kCGBitmapByteOrderDefault,//
bitmap info
                                    provider,      //
CGDataProviderRef
                                    NULL,          //decode
                                    false,         //should
interpolate
                                    kCGRenderingIntentDefault
//intent
                                    );

    // Getting UIImage from CGImage
    UIImage *finalImage = [UIImage imageWithCGImage:imageRef];
    CGImageRelease(imageRef);
    CGDataProviderRelease(provider);
    CGColorSpaceRelease(colorSpace);

    return finalImage;
}

void UIImageToMat(const UIImage* image, cv::Mat& m,
                        bool alphaExist = false)
{
    CGColorSpaceRef colorSpace = CGImageGetColorSpace(image.
CGImage);
    CGFloat cols = image.size.width, rows = image.size.height;
    CGContextRef contextRef;
    CGBitmapInfo bitmapInfo = kCGImageAlphaPremultipliedLast;
    if (CGColorSpaceGetModel(colorSpace) == 0)
    {
        m.create(rows, cols, CV_8UC1);
        //8 bits per component, 1 channel
        bitmapInfo = kCGImageAlphaNone;
        if (!alphaExist)
            bitmapInfo = kCGImageAlphaNone;
        contextRef = CGBitmapContextCreate(m.data, m.cols, m.rows,
8,
```

```
                                      m.step[0], colorSpace,
                                      bitmapInfo);
    }
    else
    {
        m.create(rows, cols, CV_8UC4); // 8 bits per component, 4
channels
        if (!alphaExist)
            bitmapInfo = kCGImageAlphaNoneSkipLast |
            kCGBitmapByteOrderDefault;
        contextRef = CGBitmapContextCreate(m.data, m.cols, m.rows,
8,
                                      m.step[0], colorSpace,
                                      bitmapInfo);
    }
    CGContextDrawImage(contextRef, CGRectMake(0, 0, cols, rows),
                        image.CGImage);
    CGContextRelease(contextRef);
}
```

5. These functions are included into the library starting from Version 2.4.6 of OpenCV. In order to use them, you should include the `ios.h` header file.

    ```
    #import "opencv2/highgui/ios.h"
    ```

6. We won't explain these functions in this recipe, because it requires from readers some knowledge about `CGImage` and `UIImage` classes; but the use of these methods is really simple. Let's consider a simple example that extracts edges from the image. In order to do so, you have to add the following code to the `viewDidLoad()` method:

    ```
    - (void)viewDidLoad
    {
        [super viewDidLoad];

        UIImage* image = [UIImage imageNamed:@"lena.png"];
        // Convert UIImage* to cv::Mat
        UIImageToMat(image, cvImage);
        if (!cvImage.empty())
        {
            cv::Mat gray;
            // Convert the image to grayscale
            cv::cvtColor(cvImage, gray, CV_RGBA2GRAY);
            // Apply Gaussian filter to remove small edges
            cv::GaussianBlur(gray, gray,
                            cv::Size(5, 5), 1.2, 1.2);
    ```

```
            // Calculate edges with Canny
            cv::Mat edges;
            cv::Canny(gray, edges, 0, 50);
            // Fill image with white color
            cvImage.setTo(cv::Scalar::all(255));
            // Change color on edges
            cvImage.setTo(cv::Scalar(0, 128, 255, 255), edges);
            // Convert cv::Mat to UIImage* and show the resulting
    image
            imageView.image = MatToUIImage(cvImage);
        }
    }
```

Now run your application and check whether the application finds edges on the image correctly.

How it works...

Frameworks are intended to simplify the process of handling dependencies. They encapsulate header and binary files, so the Xcode sees them, and you don't need to add all the paths manually. Simply speaking, the iOS framework is just a specially structured folder containing `include` files and static libraries for different architectures (for example, `armv7`, `armv7s`, and `x86`). But Xcode knows where to search for proper binaries for each build configuration, so this approach is the simplest way to link external library on the iOS. All dependencies are handled automatically and added to the final application package.

Usually, iOS applications are written in Objective-C language. Header files have a `*.h` extension and source files have `*.m`. Objective-C is a superset of C, so you can easily mix these languages in one file. But OpenCV is primarily written in C++, so we need to use C++ in the iOS project, and we need to enable support of Objective-C++. That's why we have set the language property to Objective-C++. Source files in Objective-C++ language usually have the `*.mm` extension.

To include OpenCV header files, we use the `#import` directive. It is very similar to `#include` in C++, while there is one distinction. It automatically adds guards for the included file, while in C++ we usually add them manually:

```
#ifndef __SAMPLE_H__
#define __SAMPLE_H__

...

#endif
```

In the code of the example, we just convert the loaded image from a `UIImage` object to `cv::Mat` by calling the `UIImageToMat` function. Please be careful with this function, because it entails a memory copy, so frequent calls to this function will negatively affect your application's performance.

Please note that this is probably the most important performance tip—to be very careful while working with memory in mobile applications. Avoid memory reallocations and copying as much as possible. Images require quite large chunks of memory, and you should reuse them between iterations. For example, if your application has some pipeline, you should preallocate all buffers and use the same memory while processing new frames.

After converting images, we do some simple image processing with OpenCV. First, we convert our image to the single-channel one. After that, we use the `GaussianBlur` filter to remove small details. Then we use the `Canny` method to detect edges in the image. To visualize results, we create a white image and change the color of the pixels that lie on detected edges. The resulting `cv::Mat` object is converted back to `UIImage` and displayed on the screen.

There's more...

The following is additional advice.

Objective-C++

There is one more way to add support of Objective-C++ to your project. You should just change the extension of the source files to `.mm` where you plan to use C++ code. This extension is specific to Objective-C++ code.

Converting to cv::Mat

If you don't want to use `UIImage`, but want to load an image to `cv::Mat` directly, you can do it using the following code:

```
// Create file handle
NSFileHandle* handle =
    [NSFileHandle fileHandleForReadingAtPath:filePath];
// Read content of the file
NSData* data = [handle readDataToEndOfFile];
// Decode image from the data buffer
cvImage = cv::imdecode(cv::Mat(1, [data length], CV_8UC1,
                       (void*)data.bytes),
                       CV_LOAD_IMAGE_UNCHANGED);
```

In this example we read the file content to the buffer and call the `cv::imdecode` function to decode the image. But there is one important note; if you later want to convert `cv::Mat` to the `UIImage`, you should change the channel order from BGR to RGB, as OpenCV's native image format is BGR.

Detecting faces with Cascade Classifier (Intermediate)

In this recipe, we'll learn how to detect faces using the `cv::CascadeClassifier` class from OpenCV. In order to do that, we will load an XML file with a trained classifier, use it to detect faces, and then draw a rectangle over the detected face.

Getting ready

Source code for this recipe can be found in the `Recipe04_DetectingFaces` folder in the code bundle that accompanies this book. For this recipe, you will need to download the XML file from the OpenCV sources at `http://bit.ly/3848_FaceCascade`. Alternatively, you can find the file in the resources for this book. You can use the iOS Simulator to work on this recipe.

How to do it...

The following are the basic steps needed to accomplish the task:

1. Add an XML file with cascade to the application's resources.
2. Create the `cv::CascadeClassifier` class using the cascade file from resources.
3. Detect a face on an image.
4. Draw a rectangle over the detected face.

Let's implement the described steps:

1. You can add an XML file by using the **Add Files to ...** context menu described in the *Displaying an image from resources (Simple)* recipe. Then you need to open `ViewController.h` and add a field of the `cv::CascadeClassifier` type; this will be our object detector:

   ```
   @interface ViewController : UIViewController {
       cv::CascadeClassifier faceDetector;
   }
   ```

2. The remaining steps may be implemented using the following code for the `viewDidLoad` method. Please add it to your application, then run and check if Lena's face is detected successfully:

   ```
   - (void)viewDidLoad
   {
       [super viewDidLoad];

       // Load cascade classifier from the XML file
   ```

```
        NSString* cascadePath = [[NSBundle mainBundle]
                        pathForResource:@"haarcascade_frontalface_
    alt2"
                                ofType:@"xml"];
        faceDetector.load([cascadePath UTF8String]);

        // Load image with face
        UIImage* image = [UIImage imageNamed:@"lena.png"];
        cv::Mat faceImage;
        UIImageToMat(image, faceImage);

        // Convert to grayscale
        cv::Mat gray;
        cvtColor(faceImage, gray, CV_BGR2GRAY);

        // Detect faces
        std::vector<cv::Rect> faces;
        faceDetector.detectMultiScale(gray, faces, 1.1,
                                2, 0|CV_HAAR_SCALE_IMAGE,
    cv::Size(30, 30));

        // Draw all detected faces
        for(unsigned int i = 0; i < faces.size(); i++)
        {
            const cv::Rect& face = faces[i];
            // Get top-left and bottom-right corner points
            cv::Point tl(face.x, face.y);
            cv::Point br = tl + cv::Point(face.width, face.height);

            // Draw rectangle around the face
            cv::Scalar magenta = cv::Scalar(255, 0, 255);
            cv::rectangle(faceImage, tl, br, magenta, 4, 8, 0);
        }

        // Show resulting image
        imageView.image = MatToUIImage(faceImage);
    }
```

How it works...

The first steps of this example are similar to ones from previous recipes. You should create an Xcode project, add the OpenCV framework, add a UIImageView component to the storyboard, and load an input image from the project resources. We just add some more complex OpenCV functionality to detect faces.

In the next recipes, we will discuss how to detect faces in a live video stream, but right now, let's try to do it for a static image. For this task, we use the `cv::CascadeClassifier` class. The Haar-based OpenCV face detector was initially proposed by Paul Viola and later extended by Rainer Lienhart. It is based on Haar features and allows finding some specific objects. This method is the de facto standard for face detection tasks. The input XML file contains parameters of such classifiers trained to detect frontal faces.

To load parameters, we need to convert the `NSString` object to `std::string`. In order to do it, we use the `UTF8String` method that returns a null-terminated UTF-8 representation of the `NSString` object.

After that, we can find faces on our image with the help of the `detectMultiScale` method of the `cv::CascadeClassifier` class.

OpenCV function. This function receives the following parameters to configure the detection stage:

- `scaleFactor`: This specifies how much the image size is decreased at each iteration.

- `minNeighbors`: This specifies how many neighbors each candidate rectangle should have to retain it. Increasing the value of this parameter helps to reduce the number of false positives.

- `CV_HAAR_SCALE_IMAGE`: This is a flag that specifies the algorithm to scale the image rather than the detector. It helps to achieve the best possible performance.

- `minSize`: This parameter specifies the minimum possible face size.

Detailed description of the function arguments you can be found in the OpenCV documentation at `http://bit.ly/3848_DetectMultiScale`.

This function is parallelized with Grand Central Dispatch, so it will work faster on multi-core devices.

Each detected rectangle is added to the resulting image with the `cv::rectangle` function.

There's more...

Now you can try to replace `lena.png` with your family photo or some other image with faces.

Object detection is a wide and deep subject, and we only scratched its surface in this recipe. The following will give you some pointers if you want to know more.

Native iOS face detector

The iOS Core Image framework already contains a class for face detection called `CIDetector`. So if you only need to detect faces, it can be appropriate. But the `cv::CascadeClassifier` class has more options; it can be used to detect any textured objects (with some assumptions) after training.

Detecting other types of objects

OpenCV has several trained classifiers, including frontal and profile human faces, individual facial features, silverware, and some others (more details can be found at `http://bit.ly/3848_Cascades`). You should check the available classifiers, as they might be useful in your future applications.

If there is no classifier for a particular type of object, you can always train your own, following the instructions found at `http://bit.ly/3848_TrainCascade`. But please note that training a good detector could be a challenging research task.

Tuning performance of the detector

Cascade Classifier may be too slow for real-time processing, especially on a mobile device. But there are several ways to improve the situation. First of all, please note that downscaling an image may not help, as the `detectMultiScale` method builds a pyramid of scales depending on `minSize` and `maxSize` parameters. But you can tweak these parameters to achieve better performance. Start from increasing the value of the first parameter. Next, you can try to increase the `scaleFactor` parameter. Try to use values such as `1.2` or `1.3`, but please note that it may negatively affect the quality of detection!

Apart from parameter tuning, you can try more radical methods. First of all, check if LBP-based cascade is available for your objects (`http://bit.ly/3848_LBPCascades`). **Local Binary Patterns** (**LBP**) features use integer arithmetic; thus they are more efficient and the detector usually works 2-3 times faster than using classic Haar-features (they use floating-point calculations). Finally, you can try to skip the frames in the video stream and track objects with Optical Flow between detections.

Printing a postcard (Intermediate)

In this recipe, we'll discuss how you can use your C++ classes from the Objective-C code. We'll create a simple application that prints a pretty postcard using the image with a face. We will also learn how to measure the processing time of your methods, so that you can track their efficiency.

The following screenshot shows the resulting postcard:

Getting ready

The source code for this recipe is in the `Recipe05_PrintingPostcard` folder in the code bundle that accompanies this book, where you may find implementation of the `PostcardPrinter` class and images that are going to be used in our application. You can use the iOS Simulator to work on this recipe.

How to do it...

The following is how we can implement a postcard printing application:

1. Take the application skeleton from the previous recipe.
2. Add header and implementation files of your C++ class to the Xcode project.
3. Add the calling code for the postcard printing.
4. Add time measurements and logging for the printing function.

Let's implement the described steps:

1. We will first create a new project for our application, and to save time, you can use code from the previous recipe.

2. Next, we need to add `PostcardPrinter.hpp` header file with the following class declaration:

```
class PostcardPrinter
{
public:
    struct Parameters
    {
        cv::Mat face;
        cv::Mat texture;
        cv::Mat text;
    };

    PostcardPrinter(Parameters& parameters);
    virtual ~PostcardPrinter() {}

    void print(cv::Mat& postcard) const;

protected:
    void markup();
    void crumple(cv::Mat& image, const cv::Mat& texture,
                const cv::Mat& mask = cv::Mat()) const;
    void printFragment(cv::Mat& placeForFragment,
                    const cv::Mat& fragment) const;
    void alphaBlendC3(const cv::Mat& src, cv::Mat& dst,
                    const cv::Mat& alpha) const;

    Parameters params_;
    cv::Rect faceRoi_;
    cv::Rect textRoi_;
};
```

3. Then, we need to implement all the methods of the `PostcardPrinter` class. We'll consider only `print`, `crumple`, and `printFragment` methods, because others are trivial.

```
void PostcardPrinter::printFragment(Mat& placeForFragment,
                                    const Mat& fragment) const
{
    // Get alpha channel
```

```
        vector<Mat> fragmentPlanes;
        split(fragment, fragmentPlanes);
        CV_Assert(fragmentPlanes.size() == 4);
        Mat alpha = fragmentPlanes[3];
        fragmentPlanes.pop_back();
        Mat bgrFragment;
        merge(fragmentPlanes, bgrFragment);

        // Add fragment with crumpling and alpha
        crumple(bgrFragment, placeForFragment, alpha);
        alphaBlendC3(bgrFragment, placeForFragment, alpha);
    }

    void PostcardPrinter::print(Mat& postcard) const
    {
        postcard = params_.texture.clone();

        Mat placeForFace = postcard(faceRoi_);
        Mat placeForText = postcard(textRoi_);

        printFragment(placeForFace, params_.face);
        printFragment(placeForText, params_.text);
    }

    void PostcardPrinter::crumple(Mat& image, const Mat& texture,
                                  const Mat& mask) const
    {
        Mat relief;
        cvtColor(texture, relief, CV_BGR2GRAY);
        relief = 255 - relief;

        Mat hsvImage;
        cvtColor(image, hsvImage, CV_BGR2HSV);

        vector<Mat> planes;
        split(hsvImage, planes);
        subtract(planes[2], relief, planes[2], mask);
        merge(planes, hsvImage);

        cvtColor(hsvImage, image, CV_HSV2BGR);
    }
```

4. Now we're ready to use our class from Objective-C code. We will also measure how long it takes to print the postcard and log this information to the console. Let's use the following implementation of the `viewDidLoad` method:

```objc
-  (void)viewDidLoad
{
    [super viewDidLoad];

    PostcardPrinter::Parameters params;

    // Load image with face
    UIImage* image = [UIImage imageNamed:@"lena.jpg"];
    UIImageToMat(image, params.face);

    // Load image with texture
    image = [UIImage imageNamed:@"texture.jpg"];
    UIImageToMat(image, params.texture);
    cvtColor(params.texture, params.texture, CV_RGBA2RGB);

    // Load image with text
    image = [UIImage imageNamed:@"text.png"];
    UIImageToMat(image, params.text, true);

    // Create PostcardPrinter class
    PostcardPrinter postcardPrinter(params);

    // Print postcard, and measure printing time
    cv::Mat postcard;
    int64 timeStart = cv::getTickCount();
    postcardPrinter.print(postcard);
    int64 timeEnd = cv::getTickCount();
    float durationMs =
        1000.f * float(timeEnd - timeStart) /
cv::getTickFrequency();
    NSLog(@"Printing time = %.3fms", durationMs);

    if (!postcard.empty())
        imageView.image = MatToUIImage(postcard);
}
```

You can now build and run your application to see the result.

How it works...

You can see that the `PostcardPrinter` class is an ordinary C++ class, and it actually could be used in any desktop application. We won't discuss its implementation in details, as it is not iOS-specific and is implemented using simple OpenCV functions. We will only mention that the crumpling effect is implemented by changing intensity values of images, and this is done in HSV color space. We'll first calculate the value of `relief` using `texture`, and then subtract it from the intensity plane of the image (`value` channel in HSV).

In `viewDidLoad`, we first load the images. You can note that the `params.texture` member is converted to RGB color space to comply with the input format of `PostcardPrinter`. But the `params.text` is loaded with the `alpha` channel, which is later used to avoid font aliasing. The last Boolean argument in the `UIImageToMat` function indicates that we need this image to be converted with `alpha`:

```
UIImageToMat(image, params.text, true);
```

Also note that C++ code can be seamlessly called from the Objective-C code. That's why in `viewDidLoad`, we simply create a `PostcardPrinter` object and then call its methods.

Finally, note how time measurements are added. OpenCV's `getTickCount` and `getTickFrequency` functions are used. The following line of code can be used to calculate time in seconds, so we multiply it with 1000 to get the printing time in milliseconds.

```
float(timeEnd - timeStart) / cv::getTickFrequency();
```

Depending on your device, the time will vary, but it shouldn't exceed half a second, which is good enough for our use case. Later, we will not use the `getTickCount` function directly, rather we'll use helper macros:

```
#define TS(name) int64 t_##name = cv::getTickCount()
#define TE(name) printf("TIMER_" #name ": %.2fms\n", \
    1000.*((cv::getTickCount() - t_##name) / cv::getTickFrequency()))
```

It actually does the same measurement, but it greatly improves readability of the code under inspection. It allows us to measure the working time in a simple manner as shown in the following code:

```
// Print postcard
cv::Mat postcard;
TS(PostcardPrinting);
postcardPrinter.print(postcard);
TE(PostcardPrinting);
```

There's more...

Our `PostcardPrinter` class is quite simple, but you can use it to start a full-featured application. You can add more textures, effects, and fonts, so users have more freedom while designing their postcards. In the next recipe, we apply a cool vintage effect to the photo, so it looks like a real poster from the XIX century. Its OpenCV implementation is quite simple, so we leave it for self-study.

GIMP

The text for this recipe was rendered using the **GIMP** application, which is a free alternative to Photoshop. We encourage you to get familiar with this tool (or with Photoshop), if you're going to implement advanced photo effects. You can design beautiful textures and icons for your application using GIMP.

Acceleration

iOS provides several frameworks that can be used for accelerating image processing operations. The two most important ones are **Accelerate** (`http://bit.ly/3848_Accelerate`) and **CoreImage** (`http://bit.ly/3848_CoreImage`). We will work with Accelerate in the *Using the Accelerate framework (Advanced)* recipe, but we'll provide only high-level information on CoreImage because of space limitations.

The **CoreImage** framework provides you with a set of functions that allow you to enhance, filter, blend images, and even detect faces. This API is native for iOS, and it may use GPU for acceleration. So, you may find CoreImage useful for your purposes. In fact, its functionality intersects with that of OpenCV, and some photo processing applications can be developed even without linking to OpenCV. But if you want to manually tweak your effects and performance, OpenCV is the right choice.

Working with images in Gallery (Intermediate)

In this recipe, we'll learn how to work with **Gallery** and will try to apply simple photo effects from the previous recipe to an image from Gallery. Also, it is the first recipe where we meet with the **delegation pattern** and **actions** (callbacks) for GUI elements.

If you run the corresponding project, you will get the following result:

Getting ready

Source code for this recipe can be found in the Recipe06_WorkingWithGallery folder in the code bundle that accompanies this book. You can use the iOS Simulator to work on this recipe, but you will also need an image with a face in your Gallery. You can open the Safari browser on the Simulator, copy lena.png from your PC using the drag-and-drop method, then save it using the long mouse click.

How to do it...

The first steps are the same as in the previous recipes. We should create an Xcode project, reference the OpenCV framework, add the UIImageView component, and copy files with the postcard printing code.

We are going to add the possibility to print a postcard with an image from Gallery (the image should have face in it) and save the resulting image back to Gallery. The following are the steps required to do it:

1. Add `UIToolbar` and two `UIBarButtonItem` components to the GUI.

2. Implement functions in our Controller that are relevant with needed interfaces.

3. Create actions to respond to button-clicks.

4. Finally, we will implement the `printPostcard` method that wraps the call to `PostcardPrinter` class. But before the postcard printing, we will preprocess the image with the `preprocessFace` method to add a vintage effect.

Let's implement the described steps:

1. We will first update our GUI. In order to do it, we should add the `UIToolbar` component to the bottom part of the interface. As usual, we need to select the corresponding storyboard file, choose the **Toolbar** component from the **Objects** list and drag it to the View. This component already has one button. To rename it to `Load`, you should double-click on it and enter new text. After that, we have to add a **Bar Button Item** component from the **Objects** list for the second button and rename it to `Save`.

2. The following is a declaration for our Controller interface from the `ViewController.h` file:

```
@interface ViewController :
    UIViewController<UIImagePickerControllerDelegate,
                    UINavigationControllerDelegate,
                    UIPopoverControllerDelegate>
{
        UIPopoverController* popoverController;
        UIImageView* imageView;
        UIImage* postcardImage;
        cv::CascadeClassifier faceDetector;
}

@property (nonatomic, strong) IBOutlet UIImageView* imageView;
@property (nonatomic, strong) IBOutlet UIToolbar* toolbar;
@property (nonatomic, strong) UIPopoverController*
popoverController;
@property (nonatomic, weak) IBOutlet UIBarButtonItem* loadButton;
@property (nonatomic, weak) IBOutlet UIBarButtonItem* saveButton;

- (IBAction)loadButtonPressed:(id)sender;
- (IBAction)saveButtonPressed:(id)sender;

- (UIImage*)printPostcard:(UIImage*)image;

@end
```

3. Then we should connect the `IBOutlet` properties of our Controller with corresponding components on GUI. Next, we'll consider implementation for some methods of the `ViewController` class needed to load images from Gallery:

```
- (void)imagePickerController: (UIImagePickerController*)picker
    didFinishPickingMediaWithInfo:(NSDictionary *)info
{
    if ([[UIDevice currentDevice] userInterfaceIdiom] ==

UIUserInterfaceIdiomPad)
    {
        [popoverController dismissPopoverAnimated:YES];
    }
    else
    {
        [picker dismissViewControllerAnimated:YES
                                    completion:nil];
    }

    UIImage* temp =
        [info objectForKey:@"UIImagePickerControllerOriginalIma
ge"];

    postcardImage = [self printPostcard:temp];
    imageView.image = postcardImage;

    [saveButton setEnabled:YES];
}

-(void)imagePickerControllerDidCancel:
    (UIImagePickerController *)picker
{
    if ([[UIDevice currentDevice] userInterfaceIdiom] ==

UIUserInterfaceIdiomPad)
    {
        [popoverController dismissPopoverAnimated:YES];
    }
    else
    {
        [picker dismissViewControllerAnimated:YES completion:nil];
    }
}
```

4. In order to add actions (callbacks) to our buttons, we have to implement two methods describing the response to clicks. You also should connect these functions with correspondent UI components:

```objc
- (IBAction)loadButtonPressed:(id)sender
{
    if (![UIImagePickerController isSourceTypeAvailable:
                    UIImagePickerControllerSourceTypePhotoLibrary])
        return;
    UIImagePickerController* picker =
        [[UIImagePickerController alloc] init];
    picker.delegate = self;
    picker.sourceType =
        UIImagePickerControllerSourceTypePhotoLibrary;

    if ([[UIDevice currentDevice] userInterfaceIdiom] ==
UIUserInterfaceIdiomPad)
    {
        if ([self.popoverController isPopoverVisible])
        {
            [self.popoverController dismissPopoverAnimated:YES];
        }
        else
        {
            self.popoverController =
                [[UIPopoverController alloc]
                initWithContentViewController:picker];

            popoverController.delegate = self;

            [self.popoverController
             presentPopoverFromBarButtonItem:sender
             permittedArrowDirections:UIPopoverArrowDirection
Up
                            animated:YES];
        }
    }
    else
    {
        [self presentViewController:picker
                        animated:YES
                      completion:nil];
    }
}
```

```
- (IBAction) saveButtonPressed: (id) sender
{
    if (postcardImage != nil)
    {
        UIImageWriteToSavedPhotosAlbum(postcardImage, self,
                                       nil, NULL);

        // Alert window
        UIAlertView *alert = [UIAlertView alloc];
        alert = [alert initWithTitle:@"Status"
                             message:@"Saved to the Gallery!"
                            delegate:nil
                   cancelButtonTitle:@"Continue"
                   otherButtonTitles:nil];
        [alert show];
    }
}
```

5. Finally, we should implement the `printPostcard` method that wraps the call to the `PostcardPrinter` class on the Objective-C side. You can do it yourself, similar to previous recipe. Please note that we also need to use the face detector to cut the face from the image and call the `preprocessFace` method to quantize intensity levels and add a vintage effect to the image.

The remaining functions (for example, `viewDidLoad`) were not changed much, so we'll not explain them in detail.

How it works...

For loading images from Gallery, we have to use the `UIImagePickerController` class. It provides user interfaces for choosing images and videos from your device. In order to use it, we should implement several protocols in our `ViewController` class, so it becomes a delegate that conforms to these protocols. This way, it follows the so-called **delegation mechanism** that is widely used in iOS. It allows you to avoid inheriting from base classes, and instead, the delegation requires implementing a protocol with some particular methods. In our recipe, we will use three delegates for taking images from Gallery: `UIImagePickerControllerDelegate`, `UINavigationControllerDelegate`, and `UIPopoverControllerDelegate`. To implement the first protocol, we should add the `imagePickerControllerDidCancel` method that will be called if the user presses the **Cancel** button before choosing an image in Gallery. In our recipe, we are just closing the window with the user's photo in this case. We should also implement the `didFinishPickingMediaWithInfo` method that describes the application behavior if the user selects an image. In our case, we call the `printPostcard` method for the selected image and store the result to the `image` global variable.

As you may have noticed, all these functions have a conditional statement that checks whether we use iPad or iPhone. It follows the UI guidelines for iOS. On iPhone and iPod devices, it is common to use a full screen window to show photos from Gallery, but on iPad, we have to use pop-up windows. So, to close the window, we should use two different implementations for corresponding classes of devices.

In the action of the **Load** button, we should create a `UIImagePickerController` object and set the `delegate` property of this object to our `ViewController` class. It allows us to inform our Controller about the changes and invoke the created implementation of the protocol. In the case of iPhone/iPod, we should just present the Controller with the `presentViewController` method. Implementation for tablets is a bit complicated; we should create a `UIPopoverController` object and initialize it with the previously created `UIImagePickerController` object. In order to do it, we will initialize the `self.popoverController` field that is already contained in our class, because we're using delegation from `UIPopoverControllerDelegate`.

It is our first recipe, where we were working with buttons. Here we deal with another important Cocoa design pattern called **target-action**. Actions are messages (the action) that are sent to the Controller (the target) on corresponding button-clicks. In order to process button-clicks, one should catch the corresponding events. For that purpose, you should use the `IBAction` keyword. `IBAction` is a special macro that resolves to `void`, but it denotes a method that can be linked with UI components.

There's more...

If you want to know more about the delegation and actions, we recommend you to read the Cocoa's *Communicating with Objects* guide at `http://bit.ly/3848_CommunicatingWithObjects`.

All the application logic is now in place, but we'll add some features to make our application more user-friendly.

Device orientation

Our postcards assume to be shown in the portrait orientation of a device. But, by default, GUI will be rotated if you rotate your device, and the image will be inadequately stretched. To avoid this effect, we can restrict the usage of undesirable orientations.

In order to do it, we can add the following function to our implementation of the `ViewController` class:

```
- (NSInteger) supportedInterfaceOrientations
{
    // Only portrait orientation
    return UIInterfaceOrientationMaskPortrait;
}
```

In this function, you should return a bit mask, which is a result of the *bitwise OR* operation for the desired orientations flags.

Disabling buttons

In our recipe, we are using the **Save** button to write the resulting image to Gallery. But we can't do it until we print our first postcard. In this situation, we can disable the button before the first image is chosen. To deactivate the button, we should use the `setEnabled` method:

```
[saveButton setEnabled:NO];
```

Applying a retro effect (Intermediate)

In this recipe, we'll learn how one can apply a custom photo effect to images from Gallery. We will implement a "retro" filter with OpenCV, so that the photographs look old, as shown in the following screenshot:

Getting ready

The source code for this recipe can be found in the `Recipe07_ApplyingRetroEffect` folder in the code bundle that accompanies this book. You can use the iOS Simulator to work on this recipe.

How to do it...

This recipe heavily relies on the previous one, as we're going to implement the same workflow: loading images from Gallery, processing them with OpenCV, and displaying them on the screen.

The following are the steps required to apply our filter to an image from Gallery:

1. First of all, we need to implement our custom filter. We'll create the `RetroFilter` class in C++ for that purpose.

2. Then we have to modify the `ViewController` class properly, by adding appropriate fields and its initialization in the `viewDidLoad` method.

3. Finally, we'll implement the `applyFilter` method that wraps the call to the `RetroFilter` class.

Let's implement the described steps:

1. The following is a declaration from the `RetroFilter.hpp` file for a class that is going to be used for photo stylization:

```
class RetroFilter
{
public:
    struct Parameters
    {
        cv::Size frameSize;
        cv::Mat fuzzyBorder;
        cv::Mat scratches;
    };

    RetroFilter(const Parameters& params);
    virtual ~RetroFilter() {};
    void applyToPhoto(const cv::Mat& frame, cv::Mat& retroFrame);
    void applyToVideo(const cv::Mat& frame, cv::Mat& retroFrame);

protected:
    Parameters params_;

    cv::RNG rng_;
    float multiplier_;

    cv::Mat borderColor_;
    cv::Mat scratchColor_;

    std::vector<cv::Mat> sepiaPlanes_;
    cv::Mat sepiaH_;
    cv::Mat sepiaS_;
};
```

2. We'll consider implementations for two main methods from the `RetroFilter.cpp` file. The following is a constructor for the class:

```cpp
RetroFilter::RetroFilter(const Parameters& params) : rng_(time(0))
{
    params_ = params;

    multiplier_ = 1.0;

    borderColor_.create(params_.frameSize, CV_8UC1);
    scratchColor_.create(params_.frameSize, CV_8UC1);

    sepiaH_.create(params_.frameSize, CV_8UC1);
    sepiaH_.setTo(Scalar(19));
    sepiaS_.create(params_.frameSize, CV_8UC1);
    sepiaS_.setTo(Scalar(78));
    sepiaPlanes_.resize(3);
    sepiaPlanes_[0] = sepiaH_;
    sepiaPlanes_[1] = sepiaS_;

    resize(params_.fuzzyBorder, params_.fuzzyBorder,
            params_.frameSize);

    if (params_.scratches.rows < params_.frameSize.height ||
        params_.scratches.cols < params_.frameSize.width)
    {
        resize(params_.scratches, params_.scratches,
                params_.frameSize);
    }
}
```

3. And the following is the implementation of the main processing method:

```cpp
void RetroFilter::applyToPhoto(const Mat& frame, Mat& retroFrame)
{
    Mat luminance;
    cvtColor(frame, luminance, CV_BGR2GRAY);

    // Add scratches
    Scalar meanColor = mean(luminance.row(luminance.rows / 2));
    scratchColor_.setTo(meanColor * 2.0);
    int x = rng_.uniform(0, params_.scratches.cols - luminance.
cols);
    int y = rng_.uniform(0, params_.scratches.rows - luminance.
rows);
    cv::Rect roi(cv::Point(x, y), luminance.size());
```

```
            scratchColor_.copyTo(luminance, params_.scratches(roi));

            // Add fuzzy border
            borderColor_.setTo(meanColor * 1.5);
            alphaBlendC1(borderColor_, luminance, params_.fuzzyBorder);

            // Apply sepia-effect
            sepiaPlanes_[2] = luminance + 20;
            Mat hsvFrame;
            merge(sepiaPlanes_, hsvFrame);
            cvtColor(hsvFrame, retroFrame, CV_HSV2RGB);
        }
```

4. On the Objective-C side, we need to add the `RetroFilter::Parameters` member to the `ViewController` class and the `applyFilter` method with the following implementation:

```
    - (UIImage*)applyFilter:(UIImage*)inputImage;
    {
        cv::Mat frame;
        UIImageToMat(inputImage, frame);

        params.frameSize = frame.size();
        RetroFilter retroFilter(params);

        cv::Mat finalFrame;
        retroFilter.applyToPhoto(frame, finalFrame);

        return MatToUIImage(finalFrame);
    }
```

The remaining Objective-C code is based on the previous recipe, so it is not shown here.

How it works...

The only new information in this recipe is the implementation of the `RetroFilter` class. It uses popular OpenCV functions, and we will explain only its most interesting part—the `applyToPhoto` method.

This method applies a sequence of processing steps that help us to achieve a "retro" effect. The key idea is to convert an image to a monochrome color space, do all the processing in it, and eventually convert it back to RGB with the sepia effect.

Both scratches and borders are rendered with a color that depends on a mean color of the image. To avoid costly analysis of the whole image, we only look into middle row of the image:

```
Scalar meanColor = mean(luminance.row(luminance.rows / 2));
```

You can also see that we are using the `cv::RNG` class (initialized with `rng_(time(0))`) to choose a region on the image with scratches randomly. This allows us to get different patterns of scratches for different images.

Finally, we assemble back the channels of our image. We add a value of `20` to the luminance plane, so the contrast is artificially decreased. After that, we use the OpenCV `merge` function to pack color planes into the single image, then convert it to the RGB color space with the help of the `cvtColor` function.

There's more...

You can try to use your own images with scratches and borders. As before, we recommend you to use GIMP software to edit images. But please note that both `scratches.png` and `fuzzyBorder.png` should be one-channel images, because they are used as a mask and alpha channel correspondingly.

Taking photos from camera (Intermediate)

In this recipe, we will learn how we can capture images the camera. We'll use the `CvPhotoCamera` class, which is a part of OpenCV, and apply our retro effect from the previous recipe.

Getting ready

For this recipe, you will need a real iOS device, because we're going to take photos. The source code can be found in the `Recipe08_TakingPhotosFromCamera` folder in the code bundle that accompanies this book.

How to do it...

The following are the steps required to apply our filter to a photo, taken with camera app:

1. The `ViewController` interface should implement the protocol from `CvPhotoCameraDelegate`, and should have a member of the `CvPhotoCamera*` type.

2. You will also need a couple of buttons, one to start capturing (stream preview video to display), and another for taking a photo.

3. Then we have to initialize everything in the `viewDidLoad` method as usual.

4. The last step will be the processing of the captured frame in the `applyEffect` method.

Let's implement the described steps:

1. The iOS part of the OpenCV library has two classes for working with a camera: `CvPhotoCamera` and `CvVideoCamera`. The first one was designed to get static images, and we'll get familiar with it in this recipe. We should add support for a certain protocol in our Controller class for working with a camera. In our case, we use the delegate of `CvPhotoCamera`. The `ViewController` class accesses the image through the delegation from `CvPhotoCameraDelegate`:

```
@interface ViewController : UIViewController<CvPhotoCameraDelega
te>
{
    CvPhotoCamera* photoCamera;
    UIImageView* resultView;
    RetroFilter::Parameters params;
}

@property (nonatomic, strong) CvPhotoCamera* photoCamera;
@property (nonatomic, strong) IBOutlet UIImageView* imageView;
@property (nonatomic, strong) IBOutlet UIToolbar* toolbar;
@property (nonatomic, weak) IBOutlet
    UIBarButtonItem* takePhotoButton;
@property (nonatomic, weak) IBOutlet
    UIBarButtonItem* startCaptureButton;

- (IBAction)takePhotoButtonPressed:(id)sender;
- (IBAction)startCaptureButtonPressed:(id)sender;

- (UIImage*)applyEffect:(UIImage*)image;

@end
```

2. As you can see, we need to add a `CvPhotoCamera*` property in order to work with a camera. We do also add two buttons to the UI. Thus, we add two corresponding properties and two methods with `IBAction` macros. As done before, you should connect these properties and actions with the corresponding GUI elements with **Assistant editor** and storyboard files.

3. In order to work with a camera, you should add additional frameworks to the project: **AVFoundation, Accelerate, AssetsLibrary, CoreMedia, CoreVideo, CoreImage, QuartzCore**. The simplest way to do this is using project properties by navigating to **Project | Build Phases | Link Binary With Libraries**.

4. In the `viewDidLoad` method, we should initialize camera parameters.

```
photoCamera = [[CvPhotoCamera alloc]
                            initWithParentView:imageView];
photoCamera.delegate = self;
photoCamera.defaultAVCaptureDevicePosition =
                            AVCaptureDevicePositionFront;
photoCamera.defaultAVCaptureSessionPreset =
                            AVCaptureSessionPresetPhoto;
photoCamera.defaultAVCaptureVideoOrientation =
                            AVCaptureVideoOrientationPortrait;
```

5. We'll use two buttons to control the camera. The first one will have a **Start capture** caption and we'll use it to begin capturing:

```
-(IBAction)startCaptureButtonPressed:(id)sender;
{
    [photoCamera start];

    [self.view addSubview:imageView];
    [takePhotoButton setEnabled:YES];
    [startCaptureButton setEnabled:NO];
}
```

6. In order to be compliant with the protocol of `CvPhotoCameraDelegate`, we should implement two methods inside the `ViewController` class:

```
- (void)photoCamera:(CvPhotoCamera*)camera
                    capturedImage:(UIImage *)image;
{
    [camera stop];
    resultView = [[UIImageView alloc]
                    initWithFrame:imageView.bounds];

    UIImage* result = [self applyEffect:image];

    [resultView setImage:result];
    [self.view addSubview:resultView];

    [takePhotoButton setEnabled:NO];
    [startCaptureButton setEnabled:YES];
}

- (void)photoCameraCancel:(CvPhotoCamera*)camera;
{
}
```

7. Finally, we retrieve the picture in the **Take photo** button's action. In this callback, we call the camera method for taking pictures:

```
-(IBAction)takePhotoButtonPressed:(id)sender;
{
    [photoCamera takePicture];
}
```

8. Finally, we should implement the `applyEffect` function that wraps the call to the `RetroFilter` class on the Objective-C side, as discussed in the previous recipe.

How it works...

In order to work with a camera on an iOS device using OpenCV classes, you need to initialize the `CvPhotoCamera` object first and set its parameters. This is done in the `viewDidLoad` method that is called once when the View is loaded onscreen. In the initialization code, we should specify what GUI component will be used to preview the camera capture. In our case, we'll use `UIImageView` as we did before.

Our main `UIImageView` component will be used to show the video preview from the camera and help users to take a good photo. Because our app also needs to display the final result on the screen, we create another `UIImageView` to display the processed image. In order to do it, we can create the second component right from the code:

```
resultView = [[UIImageView alloc]
                    initWithFrame:imageView.bounds];
UIImage* result = [self applyEffect:image];
[resultView setImage:result];
[self.view addSubview:resultView];
```

In this code, we create the `UIImageView` component with the same size as that of manually added `imageView` property. After that, we use the `addSubview` method of the main View to add newly created components to our GUI. If we want see the camera preview results again, we should use the same method for the `imageView` property:

```
[self.view addSubview:imageView];
```

There are three important parameters for camera: `defaultAVCaptureDevicePosition`, `defaultAVCaptureSessionPreset`, and `defaultAVCaptureVideoOrientation`. The first one is designed to choose between front and back cameras of the device. The second one is used to set the image resolution. The third parameter allows you to specify the device orientation during the capturing process.

There are many possible values for the resolution; some of them are as follows:

- `AVCaptureSessionPresetHigh`
- `AVCaptureSessionPresetMedium`
- `AVCaptureSessionPresetLow`
- `AVCaptureSessionPreset352x288`
- `AVCaptureSessionPreset640x480`

For capturing static, high-resolution images, we recommend using the value of `AVCaptureSessionPresetPhoto`. The resulting resolution depends on your device, but it will be the largest possible resolution.

In order to start the capture process, we should call the `start` method of the camera object. In our sample, we'll do it in the button's action. After clicking on the button, the user will see the camera image on the screen and will be able to click on the **Take photo** button that calls the `takePicture` method.

The `CvPhotoCameraDelegate` camera protocol contains only one important method—`capturedImage`. It is executed when somebody calls the `takePicture` function and allows you to get the current frame as the function argument.

If you want to stop the camera capturing process, you should call the `stop` method.

There's more...

If you want to start capturing at the time the application is launched, you have to call the `start` method inside `viewDidAppear`:

```
- (void)viewDidAppear:(BOOL)animated
{
    [photoCamera start];
}
```

Creating a static library (Intermediate)

In this recipe we will learn how to create a static library for use in iOS applications. This is one of the classic types, and can prove as a convenient way to share your computer vision code between multiple platforms, including desktop ones. In addition to library and headers, we will also put images to the resources of the project. Our overall goal is to build a reusable library that could be linked from multiple iOS projects. The following is what it looks like in Xcode:

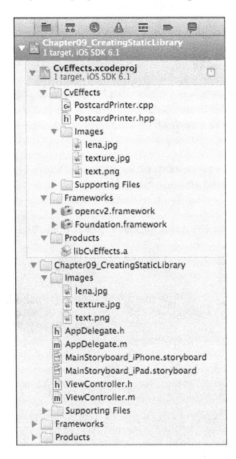

Getting ready

The source code for this recipe is available in the Recipe09_CreatingStaticLibrary and CvEffects folders in the code bundle that accompanies this book. You can use the iOS Simulator to work on this recipe.

How to do it...

This recipe is actually a refactoring of our `Recipe05_PrintingPostcard` project. We will split it into two, one will be a core computer vision library written in C++, and the second will be an iOS application, written in Objective-C.

The following is the high-level description of the required steps:

1. Create a new project of the Cocoa Touch Static Library type.
2. Reference the library project from your application project.
3. Move the source files of the `PostcardPrinter` class to the library project.
4. Add a reference to the OpenCV framework in the library project.
5. Move the images to the same project.
6. Configure your application to link the library.
7. Configure the application to use resources from the library project.

Let's implement the described steps:

1. First of all, we'll create a **Cocoa Touch Static Library** project in Xcode. Give it the name `CvEffects`, and delete the autogenerated `CvEffects.h` and `CvEffects.m` files. We'll continue to work with this project from the main application workspace, so now close library project in Xcode.

2. Now we'll add a reference to the created static library project to our application project. Create a copy of the `Recipe05_PrintingPostcard` folder in Finder, and then open the project in Xcode. Now you need to drag your `CvEffects.xcodeproj` from the Finder into the **Project Navigator Area** of the Xcode project.

3. Now select both `PostcardPrinter.hpp` and `PostcardPrinter.cpp` and drag them to the **CvEffects** group that is located under **CvEffects.xcodeproj**. In the appeared window, check both **Copy items into the destination group's folder** and **Add to targets** checkboxes. Now move the same source files to trash from the application project.

4. In order to make the header file visible to the application project, we need to set up its copying during build. Open the **Build Phases** settings window of **CvEffects. xcodeproj** and expand the **Copy Files** build phase. Then add `PostcardPrinter. hpp` to the list, as shown in the following screenshot:

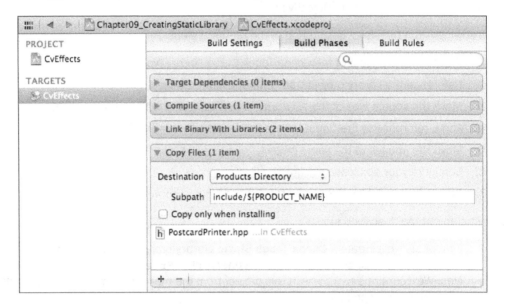

 Please note that if you're going to add new classes to the library project, they will be not visible in your main application project until you set up the copying of the headers. So, every time you update the library project, you need to update this list of public headers and rebuild the project.

5. Now add the reference to OpenCV framework as we did in the previous recipes. In the library project, create a new group called `Images`. Then in the application project, select all the images needed for postcard printing: `lena.jpg`, `texture.jpg`, and `text.png`, and drag them to the **Images** group. Make sure that you've checked the **Copy items into the destination group's folder** checkbox and unchecked the **Add to targets** checkbox. Now, move these images to trash from the application project.

6. Our library is configured properly, and it's time to link it from our application. First of all, you need to update your import to the following line:

```
#import "CvEffects/PostcardPrinter.hpp"
```

7. Then you have to open the **Build Phases** settings of the **Recipe09_ CreatingStaticLibrary.xcodeproj** project, expand the **Link Binary With Libraries** phase, and add the `libCvEffects.lib` library, as shown in the following screenshot:

Instant OpenCV for iOS

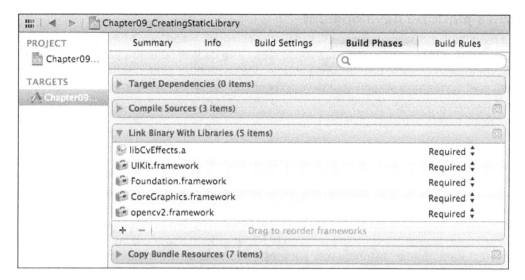

8. Finally, you need to add references to images. First, create the **Images** group as a subgroup of **Recipe09_CreatingStaticLibrary.xcodeproj**. Then select all three images in the library project, and drag them to the created **Images** group. In the window that appears, uncheck the **Copy items into the destination group's folder** checkbox (as we want application to reference images from the library project), and check the **Add to targets** checkbox.

The setup is complete; now you can build and run the application.

How it works...

The static library project on iOS doesn't differ much from the static libraries for other platforms, so we'll not dig deeper into this subject. As you can see, such project type allows you not only to keep the source files, but also to keep the images and other resources. This is a good opportunity to reduce duplication in your code base.

There's more...

For a more detailed introduction into static libraries in iOS, you can refer to the official documentation at `http://bit.ly/3848_iOSStaticLibraries`.

A static library is a good way to reuse your code between projects, but there are some additional opportunities for developers. Let's discuss them.

49

Cross-platform development

The described approach allows you to isolate the computer vision logic from the user interface and user interaction logic. This allows you to reuse your code in other iOS projects, but more importantly, you can also use the same library code on multiple platforms, including desktop. This could significantly simplify your development and debugging processes. It is generally a good practice to initially develop the computer vision logic on a desktop computer, because debugging may be a tricky problem.

Frameworks

One of drawbacks of static libraries is that they require some work from users, as they need to add header files and the library to the linking process. iOS provides a more convenient way when you wrap your code into a framework. As a result, user just points to the framework in the Xcode, and all dependencies are added automatically. This is actually how OpenCV is distributed. We will not cover the creation of frameworks in this book, but please keep in mind that if you want to distribute your libraries, you should consider this approach, as it simplifies the life of your users. The Xcode community has created several Xcode templates that could help you start; they can be found at `https://github.com/kstenerud/iOS-Universal-Framework`.

Capturing a video from camera (Simple)

In this recipe, we will use the `CvVideoCamera` class to capture live video from camera.

Getting ready

The source code can be found in the `Recipe10_CapturingVideo` folder in the code bundle that accompanies this book. For this recipe, you can't use Simulator, as it doesn't support camera.

How to do it...

The high-quality camera, in the latest iOS devices, is one of important factors of the popularity of these devices. The ability to capture and encode H.264 high-definition video with hardware acceleration was accepted with great enthusiasm by users and developers.

Most of the functions related to communicating with camera are included in the **AVFoundation** framework. This framework contains a lot of simple and easy-to-use classes for taking photos and videos. But setting up a camera, retrieving frames, displaying them, and handling rotations, take a lot of code. So, in this recipe, we will use the `CvVideoCamera` class from OpenCV, which encapsulates the functionality of the AVFoundation framework.

The following are the steps required to capture video on iOS:

1. The `ViewController` interface should implement the protocol from `CvVideoCameraDelegate`, and should have a member of the `CvVideoCamera*` type.

2. You will also need a couple of buttons, one to start capturing process (stream preview video to display), and second to stop the process.

3. Then we have to initialize everything in the `viewDidLoad` method as usual.

4. Finally, we'll implement the camera control with GUI buttons.

Let's implement the described steps:

1. Similar to the *Taking photos from camera (Intermediate)* recipe, in order to work with camera, we need to implement a specific protocol (`CvVideoCameraDelegate`) in our `ViewController` class. We also should include the special header file with interfaces of the OpenCV camera classes.

```
#import <opencv2/highgui/ios.h>

@interface ViewController : UIViewController<CvVideoCameraDelega
te>
{
    CvVideoCamera* videoCamera;
    BOOL isCapturing;
}

@property (nonatomic, strong) CvVideoCamera* videoCamera;
@property (nonatomic, strong) IBOutlet UIImageView* imageView;
@property (nonatomic, strong) IBOutlet UIToolbar* toolbar;
@property (nonatomic, weak) IBOutlet
    UIBarButtonItem* startCaptureButton;
@property (nonatomic, weak) IBOutlet
    UIBarButtonItem* stopCaptureButton;

- (IBAction) startCaptureButtonPressed:(id)sender;
- (IBAction) stopCaptureButtonPressed:(id)sender;

@end
```

2. We will need two buttons, so we have to add two corresponding properties and two methods with IBAction macros. As before, you should connect these properties and actions with corresponding GUI elements using **Assistant** editor and storyboard files:

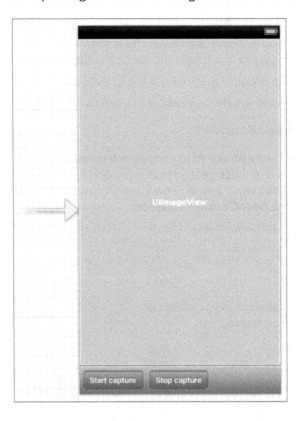

3. In order to work with the camera, you should add additional frameworks to the project: AVFoundation, Accelerate, AssetsLibrary, CoreMedia, CoreVideo, CoreImage, and QuartzCore. The simplest way to do this is using project properties by navigating to **Project | Build Phases | Link Binary With Libraries**.

4. In the viewDidLoad method, we should initialize the camera parameters:

```
- (void)viewDidLoad
{
    [super viewDidLoad];

    self.videoCamera = [[CvVideoCamera alloc]
                            initWithParentView:imageView];
    self.videoCamera.delegate = self;
    self.videoCamera.defaultAVCaptureDevicePosition =
                            AVCaptureDevicePositionFront;
```

```
        self.videoCamera.defaultAVCaptureSessionPreset =
                                AVCaptureSessionPreset640x480;
        self.videoCamera.defaultAVCaptureVideoOrientation =
                                AVCaptureVideoOrientationPortrait;
        self.videoCamera.defaultFPS = 30;

        isCapturing = NO;
    }
```

5. We'll use the first button with the **Start capture** caption to begin capturing from camera, and the other one with the **Stop capture** caption to stop:

```
    -(IBAction)startCaptureButtonPressed:(id)sender
    {
        [videoCamera start];
        isCapturing = YES;
    }


    -(IBAction)stopCaptureButtonPressed:(id)sender
    {
        [videoCamera stop];
        isCapturing = NO;
    }
```

6. To monitor the status of the capturing process, we'll use the `isCapturing` variable, which would be set to `YES` when capturing is active and `NO` otherwise.

7. According to the `CvVideoCameraDelegate` protocol, our `ViewController` class needs to implement a `processImage` method (handle the `processImage` message).

```
    -  (void)processImage:(cv::Mat&)image
    {
        // Do some OpenCV processing with the image
    }
```

8. Finally, you can add some code to this method for processing video on the fly; we will do it in another recipe.

How it works...

As we mentioned earlier, the iOS part of the OpenCV library has two classes for working with camera: `CvPhotoCamera` and `CvVideoCamera`. The difference between the two classes is rather conventional. The first one was designed to only capture static images and you can process images only after capturing them (offline mode). The other class provides more opportunities. It can capture video, process it on the fly, and save the processed stream as an H.264 video file. Those classes have a quite similar interface and are inherited from the common `CvAbstractCamera` ancestor.

The CvVideoCamera class is easy to use. You can leave the default values for resolution, **frames-per-second** (**FPS**), and so on, or customize them when needed. The parameters are the same as the ones in the CvPhotoCamera class; however, there is one new parameter called defaultFPS. Usually, this value is chosen between 20 and 30; 30 being standard for video.

Previously, we recommended using AVCaptureSessionPresetPhoto as a resolution parameter of the CvPhotoCamera class. In case of video capturing, the better way is to choose a smaller resolution. In order to do so, you can use one of the fixed resolutions (for example, AVCaptureSessionPreset640x480, AVCaptureSessionPreset1280x720, and so on) or one of the relative ones (AVCaptureSessionPresetHigh, AVCaptureSessionPresetMedium, and AVCaptureSessionPresetLow). The resulting resolution in the latter case will depend on the respective device and camera. Some of the values are listed in the following table:

Preset	iPhone 3G	iPhone 3GS	iPhone 4 back	iPhone 4 front
AVCaptureSession PresetHigh	400 x 304	640 x 480	1280 x 720	640 x 480
AVCaptureSession PresetMedium	400 x 304	480 x 360	480 x 360	480 x 360
AVCaptureSession PresetMedium	400 x 304	192 x 144	192 x 144	192 x 144

Using the lowest possible resolution and reasonable frame rate can save a lot of power and make apps more responsive. So, set up your camera preview resolution and FPS to the lowest reasonable values.

To work with camera on an iOS device using the OpenCV class, you should first initialize the CvVideoCamera object and set its parameters; you can do it in the viewDidLoad method.

In order to start the capturing process, we should call the start method of the camera object. In our sample, we'll do it in the button's actions (callback functions). After pressing the button, the user will see the camera preview on the screen. In order to stop capturing, you should call the stop method. You should also implement the processImage method that allows you to process camera images on the fly; this method will be called for each frame. Its input parameter is already converted to cv::Mat that simplifies calling the OpenCV functions.

It is also recommended to stop the camera when the application is closing. Add the following code to guarantee that the camera stops in case the user doesn't click on the **Stop capture** button:

```
- (void)viewDidDisappear:(BOOL)animated
{
    [super viewDidDisappear:animated];
```

```
    if (isCapturing) {
        [videoCamera stop];
    }
}
```

There's more...

`CvVideoCamera` simply wraps AVFoundation functions. So, if you need more control on the camera, you should use this framework directly. The other way is to add OpenCV classes for working with the camera to your project directly. For that purpose, you should copy `cap_ios_abstract_camera.mm`, `cap_ios_photo_camera.mm`, `cap_ios_video_camera.mm`, and `cap_ios.h` from the `highgui` module and modify the included files. You will need to rename the classes to avoid conflict with the classes of OpenCV.

Real-time video processing on mobile devices is often a computationally intensive task, so it is recommended to use dedicated frameworks, such as Accelerate and CoreImage. Such frameworks are highly optimized and accelerated with special hardware, so you can expect decent processing time and significant power savings.

Control advanced camera settings (Advanced)

In computer vision, we often should calibrate the camera of a device and find its intrinsic and extrinsic parameters (**pinhole camera model**). In order to do this, we should have the possibility to lock some camera settings (for example, focus) to calculate the camera parameters as accurately as possible. In this recipe, we'll consider some advanced settings provided by the `CvVideoCamera` class that can help you during the calibration process.

Getting ready

We will use the `Recipe10_CapturingVideo` project as a starting point, trying to add more control over the iOS camera. The source code can be found in the `Recipe11_AdvancedCameraControl` folder in the code bundle that accompanies this book. For this recipe you can't use Simulator, as it doesn't support camera.

How to do it...

The following are the required steps:

1. Add four buttons to our GUI to control the focus, exposure, white balance, and camera rotation.

2. Then implement actions for all buttons.

Let's implement the described steps:

1. Similarly to previous recipe, we should implement basic functions to work with the video camera and add four more buttons to our UI:

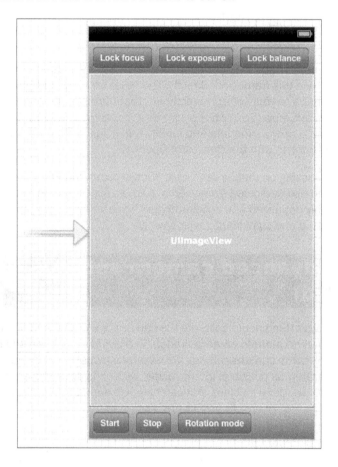

```
#import <opencv2/highgui/ios.h>

@interface ViewController : UIViewController<CvVideoCameraDelega
te>
{
    CvVideoCamera* videoCamera;
    BOOL isCapturing;
    BOOL isFocusLocked, isExposureLocked, isBalanceLocked;
}

@property (nonatomic, strong) CvVideoCamera* videoCamera;
```

```
@property (nonatomic, strong) IBOutlet UIImageView* imageView;
@property (nonatomic, strong) IBOutlet UIToolbar* toolbar;
@property (nonatomic, weak) IBOutlet
    UIBarButtonItem* startCaptureButton;
@property (nonatomic, weak) IBOutlet
    UIBarButtonItem* stopCaptureButton;

@property (nonatomic, weak) IBOutlet
    UIBarButtonItem* lockFocusButton;
@property (nonatomic, weak) IBOutlet
    UIBarButtonItem* lockExposureButton;
@property (nonatomic, weak) IBOutlet
    UIBarButtonItem* lockBalanceButton;
@property (nonatomic, weak) IBOutlet
    UIBarButtonItem* rotationButton;

-(IBAction)startCaptureButtonPressed:(id)sender;
-(IBAction)stopCaptureButtonPressed:(id)sender;

- (IBAction)actionLockFocus:(id)sender;
- (IBAction)actionLockExposure:(id)sender;
- (IBAction)actionLockBalance:(id)sender;

- (IBAction)rotationButtonPressed:(id)sender;

@end
```

2. Then, the first three buttons will be used to control the focus, exposure, and white balance settings. These buttons will have two modes: locked and unlocked. In order to do it, we should implement the corresponding actions:

```
- (IBAction)actionLockFocus:(id)sender
{
    if (isFocusLocked)
    {
        [self.videoCamera unlockFocus];
        [lockFocusButton setTitle:@"Lock focus"];
        isFocusLocked = NO;
    }
    else
    {
        [self.videoCamera lockFocus];
        [lockFocusButton setTitle:@"Unlock focus"];
        isFocusLocked = YES;
    }
```

```
    }

-   (IBAction)actionLockExposure:(id)sender
    {
        if (isExposureLocked)
        {
            [self.videoCamera unlockExposure];
            [lockExposureButton setTitle:@"Lock exposure"];
            isExposureLocked = NO;
        }
        else
        {
            [self.videoCamera lockExposure];
            [lockExposureButton setTitle:@"Unlock exposure"];
            isExposureLocked = YES;
        }
    }


-   (IBAction)actionLockBalance:(id)sender
    {
        if (isBalanceLocked)
        {
            [self.videoCamera unlockBalance];
            [lockBalanceButton setTitle:@"Lock balance"];
            isBalanceLocked = NO;
        }
        else
        {
            [self.videoCamera lockBalance];
            [lockBalanceButton setTitle:@"Unlock balance"];
            isBalanceLocked = YES;
        }
    }
```

3. The remaining fourth button will change the camera image orientation relative to the device orientation. It has two possible modes, and we just change the current mode in the action:

```
-   (IBAction)rotationButtonPressed:(id)sender
    {
        videoCamera.rotateVideo = !videoCamera.rotateVideo;
    }
```

How it works...

First, let's investigate the focus changing on iOS devices. The iOS camera API supports three modes for camera focus:

- ▸ `AVCaptureFocusModeLocked`: When enabled, the focus becomes fixed.
- ▸ `AVCaptureFocusModeAutoFocus`: When enabled, the camera performs an autofocus operation and then returns to the locked mode.
- ▸ `AVCaptureFocusModeContinuousAutoFocus`: When enabled, the camera continuously monitors focus and autofocuses as needed.

`CvVideoCamera` uses the `AVCaptureFocusModeContinuousAutoFocus` mode by default, so the focus may change with the scene. This can make the process of camera calibration much more difficult. The best way, in this case, is to set the focus to some special value (for example, infinity), but unfortunately, the iOS API doesn't contain all functions needed by computer vision specialists. There is no way to programmatically set the camera focus of an iOS device to infinity or any other predefined value. So we can only lock the current focus value. For that purpose, the `CvVideoCamera` class provides the `lockFocus` method. It changes the focus mode to the `AVCaptureFocusModeLocked` value. In order to unlock it again, you should use the `unlockFocus` function.

You can also control the exposure and white balance in the same way using `lockExposure` and `lockBalance` functions.

To control image rotation in camera, you can change the `rotateVideo` property. The default value of this variable is `NO`.

 In previous OpenCV versions the default value was `YES`.

In this mode, the camera image will not be rotated with the device rotation. If you change this value, the image will be rotated every time a device changes its orientation by 90 degrees.

Each newly added button in this project allows you to switch between the two modes. To indicate mode changing, we'll change the button's text. For that purpose, you can use the `setTitle` method.

There's more...

AVFoundation contains a lot of useful functions for advanced control of the iOS camera. For example, you can get exposure time for each frame. If you need such fine-grain control, you should work with AVFoundation directly.

Applying effects to live video (Intermediate)

In this recipe, we'll consider an example showing how to take a live video feed and apply an image filter in real-time. As we discussed previously, you should only implement the processImage method. Also, we'll add displaying the FPS number directly in camera images, it can help you in the optimization process. The following is an example snapshot of the application:

Getting ready

We will use the Recipe10_CapturingVideo project as a starting point, trying to apply previously implemented RetroFilter to the video stream. We also suppose that the RetroFilter class, and its resources were added to the CvEffects static library project. Source code can be found in the Recipe12_ProcessingVideo folder in the code bundle that accompanies this book. For this recipe, you can't use Simulator, as it doesn't support working with camera.

How to do it...

The following are the required steps:

1. Add instance variables for storing retro filter properties.

2. Add an initialization of the filter to the button's action.

3. Finally, we'll implement applying the filter in the `processImage` function.

Let's implement the described steps:

1. First, we should add the `RetroFilter::Parameters` variable and a pointer to the filter to the Controller interface. Also, we'll add a variable for storing the previous time for FPS calculation:

   ```
   @interface ViewController : UIViewController<CvVideoCameraDelega
   te>
   {
       CvVideoCamera* videoCamera;
       BOOL isCapturing;
       RetroFilter::Parameters params;
       cv::Ptr<RetroFilter> filter;
       uint64_t prevTime;
   }
   ```

2. In order to initialize filter properties, we should add some code to the `viewDidLoad` function:

   ```
   // Load textures
   UIImage* resImage = [UIImage imageNamed:@"scratches.png"];
   UIImageToMat(resImage, params.scratches);

   resImage = [UIImage imageNamed:@"fuzzy_border.png"];
   UIImageToMat(resImage, params.fuzzyBorder);

   filter = NULL;
   prevTime = mach_absolute_time();
   ```

3. As we know the resolution of the camera only after session starts, we should create a filter object when the **StartCapture** button is pressed:

   ```
   -(IBAction)startCaptureButtonPressed:(id)sender
   {
       [videoCamera start];
       isCapturing = YES;

       params.frameSize = cv::Size(videoCamera.imageWidth,
   ```

```
                                          videoCamera.imageHeight);

        if (!filter)
            filter = new RetroFilter(params);
    }
```

4. Finally, we should apply the filter to a camera image:

```objc
- (void)processImage:(cv::Mat&)image
{
    cv::Mat inputFrame = image;

    BOOL isNeedRotation = image.size() != params.frameSize;
    if (isNeedRotation)
        inputFrame = image.t();

    // Apply filter
    cv::Mat finalFrame;
    filter->applyToVideo(inputFrame, finalFrame);

    if (isNeedRotation)
        finalFrame = finalFrame.t();

    // Add fps label to the frame
    uint64_t currTime = mach_absolute_time();
    double timeInSeconds = machTimeToSecs(currTime - prevTime);
    prevTime = currTime;
    double fps = 1.0 / timeInSeconds;
    NSString* fpsString =
                    [NSString stringWithFormat:@"FPS = %3.2f",
fps];
        cv::putText(finalFrame, [fpsString UTF8String],
                cv::Point(30, 30), cv::FONT_HERSHEY_COMPLEX_SMALL,
                0.8, cv::Scalar::all(255));

    finalFrame.copyTo(image);
}
```

5. We will use the following function to convert the measured time to seconds:

```objc
static double machTimeToSecs(uint64_t time)
{
    mach_timebase_info_data_t timebase;
    mach_timebase_info(&timebase);
    return (double)time * (double)timebase.numer /
                            (double)timebase.denom / 1e9;
}
```

6. As you can see, this code contains the `mach_timebase_info` structure that is defined in the following header file:

```
#import <mach/mach_time.h>
```

How it works...

In the previous cases, we always created the filter object right before using it. In the case of live video, we cannot do it, because the performance issues come out on top. So we'll initialize the `RetroFilter` object only once. For this purpose, we have to add a smart pointer, which points to the filter object, to the Controller interface and initialize it after starting the video capturing process. We can't do it in the `viewDidLoad` method, because we should know the camera resolution from before.

To calculate FPS, we have to add the `prevTime` field property. We will measure the time between `processImage` calls with this variable. At the time of the first call to this method, we'll initialize this property with the current time. During the next call, we will be able to measure the working time of the filter function, plus the time needed to get the camera image as a difference between current time and value of the `prevTime` variable. After that, we can convert it to seconds and calculate the resulting FPS value. In order to display the number on the screen, we'll use the `cv::putText` function.

There's more...

Even on the latest iOS devices (iPad 4 and iPhone 5) our filter shows good FPS (~30) only on low resolutions, for example 352 x 288. In the next recipes, we'll consider a few ways to optimize the OpenCV applications with iOS- and ARM-specific techniques.

Saving video from camera (Simple)

In the earlier recipes, we saved images, after some filtering, to Gallery as user's photos. In this recipe, we will investigate how to create a video file from camera images and save it to Gallery.

Getting ready

We will use the `Recipe12_CapturingVideo` project as a starting point, trying to add the possibility to save processed camera images as video. The source code can be found in the `Recipe13_SavingVideo` folder in the code bundle that accompanies this book. For this recipe, you can't use Simulator, as it doesn't support camera.

How to do it...

One of the many features supported by the latest iOS devices is 1080p HD video recording. It is incredible, because it is the largest resolution for the majority of modern TVs. Also, the modern iOS devices support hardware encoding with the H.264 codec and QuickTime container (.mov).

The following are the required steps:

1. Enable video recording by changing recordVideo property.
2. Add code for copying resulting video to Gallery when capturing is stopped.

Let's implement the described steps:

1. In order to enable video recording, we'll change the default value of the recordVideo property in the viewDidLoad method:

   ```
   videoCamera.recordVideo = YES;
   ```

2. After that, we will add additional code to the **Stop capture** button's action:

   ```
   -(IBAction)stopCaptureButtonPressed:(id)sender
   {
       [videoCamera stop];

       NSString* relativePath = [videoCamera.videoFileURL
   relativePath];
       UISaveVideoAtPathToSavedPhotosAlbum(relativePath, nil, NULL,
   NULL);

       //Alert window
       UIAlertView *alert = [UIAlertView alloc];
       alert = [alert initWithTitle:@"Status"
                           message:@"Saved to the Gallery!"
                          delegate:nil
                  cancelButtonTitle:@"Continue"
                  otherButtonTitles:nil];
       [alert show];

       isCapturing = FALSE;
   }
   ```

How it works...

At a high level, the main method of the `CvVideoCamera` class (that captures frames and processes them) looks like the following:

```
while (flag)
{
    if (self.delegate)
    {
        //Get current frame

        //Call process function

        if (self.recordVideo == YES) {
            //Add the image to video file
        }
    }
}
```

In other words, the `processImage` method will be called for each frame after calling the `start` method. And each processed frame is saved to the resulting video file if the value of the `recordVideo` variable is `YES`.

When a user clicks on the **Stop capture** button, the `stopCaptureButtonPressed` method is called. In this function, we have to call the `stop` method initially. After that, the resulting video file becomes available in `tmp` folder of the current application. You can copy it from device with some software, such as iFunBox. You can get the path to this file through the `videoCamera.videoFileURL` property. In order to copy it to Gallery, we should call the `UISaveVideoAtPathToSavedPhotosAlbum` function using the path to the generated file. After that, we can show an alert window with a notification message about video saving as done in the *Capturing a video from camera (Simple)* recipe.

Optimizing performance with ARM NEON (Advanced)

NEON is a set of **single instruction, multiple data** (**SIMD**) instructions for ARM, and it can help in performance optimization. In this recipe, we will learn how to add NEON support to your project, and how to vectorize the code using it.

Getting ready

We will use the `Recipe12_ProcessingVideo` project as a starting point, trying to minimize the processing time. The source code is available in the `Recipe14_OptimizingWithNEON` folder in the code bundle that accompanies this book. For this recipe, you can't use Simulator, as NEON instructions are not supported on it and they are ARM-specific, while Simulator is x86.

How to do it...

The following is how we will optimize our video processing application:

1. Profile the application and find hotspots.
2. Enable NEON support in our source code.
3. Create an alternative implementation for the bottleneck functions using NEON.

Let's implement the described steps:

1. First of all, we need to profile the `RetroFilter::applyToVideo` method, as it is the most time consuming part of our application. We'll create a copy of this method with the name `applyToVideo_optimized`, and insert time measurements in it, as we did in the *Printing a postcard (Intermediate)* recipe. We'll not show the code of the method here, as it differs with these measurements only.

 It is generally a good practice to use special profiling tools to find hotspots in an application. But in our case, we only have a few functions, and it is better to measure their individual time without using any tools. Image processing tasks are quite time consuming, so you can easily detect bottlenecks with simple logging, and focus on optimization.

2. The following is a sample console log with processing steps:

   ```
   TIMER_ConvertingToGray: 8.28ms

   TIMER_IntensityVariation: 16.23ms

   TIMER_AddingScratches: 4.46ms

   TIMER_FuzzyBorder: 14.65ms

   TIMER_ConvertingToBGR: 2.59ms

   2013-05-25 19:04:12.879 Recipe14_OptimizingWithNEON[4503:5203]
   Processing time = 48.05ms; Running average FPS = 20.1;
   ```

Profiling will show that there are two major hotspots in our application: `alphaBlendC1` function and the matrix multiplication with scalar (intensity variation). Because both functions process individual pixels independently, we can parallelize their execution. We then have several choices, such as multi-threading (via `libdispatch`) of vectorization using the NEON SIMD instruction set. To process images with several threads, we can split them into several stripes (for example, into four horizontal stripes) and process them as submatrices. This approach is quite easy to implement, and it actually doesn't require memory copy.

3. But let's focus on NEON; we will put the vectorized code to the `Processing_NEON.cpp` file of the `CvEffects` static library project. It is shown in the following code snippet:

```cpp
#include "Processing.hpp"

#if defined(__ARM_NEON__)
  #include <arm_neon.h>
#endif

#define USE_NEON true
#define USE_FIXED_POINT false

using namespace cv;

void alphaBlendC1_NEON(const Mat& src, Mat& dst, const Mat& alpha)
{
    CV_Assert(src.type() == dst.type() == alpha.type() == CV_8UC1
&&
                src.isContinuous() && dst.isContinuous() &&
                alpha.isContinuous() &&
                (src.cols % 8 == 0) &&
                (src.cols == dst.cols) && (src.cols == alpha.cols));

#if !defined(__ARM_NEON__) || !USE_NEON
    alphaBlendC1(src, dst, alpha);
#else
    uchar* pSrc = src.data;
    uchar* pDst = dst.data;
    uchar* pAlpha = alpha.data;
    for(int i=0; i < src.total(); i+=8, pSrc+=8, pDst+=8,
pAlpha+=8)
    {
        // Load data from memory to NEON registers
        uint8x8_t vsrc = vld1_u8(pSrc);
```

```
        uint8x8_t vdst = vld1_u8(pDst);
        uint8x8_t valpha = vld1_u8(pAlpha);
        uint8x8_t v255 = vdup_n_u8(255);

        // Multiply source pixels
        uint16x8_t mult1 = vmull_u8(vsrc, valpha);

        // Multiply destination pixels
        uint8x8_t tmp = vsub_u8(v255, valpha);
        uint16x8_t mult2 = vmull_u8(tmp, vdst);

        //Add them
        uint16x8_t sum = vaddq_u16(mult1, mult2);

        // Take upper bytes (approximates division by 255)
        uint8x8_t out = vshrn_n_u16(sum, 8);

        // Store the result back to the memory
        vst1_u8(pDst, out);
    }
#endif
}


void multiply_NEON(Mat& src, float multiplier)
{
    CV_Assert(src.type() == CV_8UC1 && src.isContinuous() &&
            (src.cols % 8 == 0));

#if !defined(__ARM_NEON__) || !USE_NEON
    src *= multiplier;
#elif USE_FIXED_POINT
    uchar fpMult = uchar((multiplier * 128.f) + 0.5f);
    uchar* ptr = src.data;
    for(int i = 0; i < src.total(); i+=8, ptr+=8)
    {
        uint8x8_t vsrc = vld1_u8(ptr);
        uint8x8_t vmult = vdup_n_u8(fpMult);
        uint16x8_t product = vmull_u8(vsrc, vmult);
        uint8x8_t out = vqshrn_n_u16(product, 7);
        vst1_u8(ptr, out);
    }

#else
    uchar* ptr = src.data;
    for(int i = 0; i < src.total(); i+=8, ptr+=8)
    {
```

```
        float32x4_t vmult1 = vdupq_n_f32(multiplier);
        float32x4_t vmult2 = vdupq_n_f32(multiplier);

        uint8x8_t in = vld1_u8(ptr); // Load

        // Convert to 16bit
        uint16x8_t in16bit = vmovl_u8(in);

        // Split vector
        uint16x4_t in16bit1 = vget_high_u16(in16bit);
        uint16x4_t in16bit2 = vget_low_u16(in16bit);

        // Convert to float
        uint32x4_t in32bit1 = vmovl_u16(in16bit1);
        uint32x4_t in32bit2 = vmovl_u16(in16bit2);
        float32x4_t inFlt1 = vcvtq_f32_u32(in32bit1);
        float32x4_t inFlt2 = vcvtq_f32_u32(in32bit2);

        // Multiplication
        float32x4_t outFlt1 = vmulq_f32(vmult1, inFlt1);
        float32x4_t outFlt2 = vmulq_f32(vmult2, inFlt2);

        // Convert from float
        uint32x4_t out32bit1 = vcvtq_u32_f32(outFlt1);
        uint32x4_t out32bit2 = vcvtq_u32_f32(outFlt2);
        uint16x4_t out16bit1 = vmovn_u32(out32bit1);
        uint16x4_t out16bit2 = vmovn_u32(out32bit2);

        // Combine back
        uint16x8_t out16bit = vcombine_u16(out16bit2, out16bit1);

        // Convert to 8bit
        uint8x8_t out8bit = vqmovn_u16(out16bit);

        // Store to the memory
        vst1_u8(ptr, out8bit);
    }
#endif
}
```

4. Now, we should call these functions from the `applyToVideo_optimized` method.

5. When ready, build and run the application. Depending on your device, you can see up to two times the total performance speedup. Speedup of optimized functions alone is much higher.

How it works...

Nowadays, SIMD instructions are available on many architectures, from desktop CPU to embedded DSP. ARM processors provide a rich set of instructions, called NEON; they are available on all iOS devices starting from iPhone 3GS.

To start writing NEON code, you have to add the following declaration to your file:

```
#if defined(__ARM_NEON__)
    #include <arm_neon.h>
#endif
```

Now you can use all the types and functions declared there. Please note, that we're going to use the so-called **intrinsics**—functions in C that serve as a wrapper over NEON assembler instructions. In fact, you can write your code in pure assembler, but it will worsen the readability, although there is a small performance gain, it usually isn't worth it.

Let's consider how the `alphaBlendC1_optimized` function works. This function should use the following formula to calculate the resulting pixel's value:

dst(x, y) = [alpha(x, y) * src(x, y) + (255.0 - alpha(x, y)) * dst(x, y)] / 255.0;

The NEON code does exactly that, except the very last division, which is approximated by bit-shifting 8 positions to the right (`vshrn_n_u16` function). This means that we divide by 256, instead of 255, and the result of the vectorized function may differ from the original implementation. But we can tolerate that, as we're working on a visual effect, and the possible difference is negligibly small. But please note that such approximations may be unacceptable in a numerical pipeline.

You can also see that we process 8 pixels simultaneously. Our `alphaBlendC1_optimized` function heavily relies on the exact format of input matrices (that is, is one channel, is continuous, and the number of columns is a multiple of 8), but it can be easily generalized for other situations.

 If the image width is not divided by the width of the SIMD instruction, the common practice is to process the tail with ordinary C code. As images are normally large enough, this non-vectorized processing near the right-hand side border doesn't affect performance much.

The `multiply` function performs simple multiplication with a floating-point coefficient. But we need to do a sequence of conversions to perform the multiplication. But still, because we process 8 pixels simultaneously, the speedup is impressive.

There's more...

Performance optimization with NEON is a deep and wide subject. Most image processing functions could be optimized for 3x speedup, without affecting accuracy. You can even get more if you apply some approximations. In the following sections, we provide some pointers for further study.

NEON

ARM Information Center provides extensive documentation on NEON intrinsics, and can be found at `http://bit.ly/3848_ARMNEON`. You can see that the instruction set is quite rich, and allows you to optimize your code in different situations.

Fixed-point arithmetic

Our `multiply` function is a naive translation of the C++ code to NEON intrinsics. But sometimes, it is possible to achieve much better speedup by using some approximation. The very popular method of approximating floating-point calculations is the so-called **fixed-point arithmetic**, where we store real numbers in variables of integer type (`http://en.wikipedia.org/wiki/Fixed-point_arithmetic`).

In our case, we can convert the value of `multiplier` into the Q1.7 format, perform multiplication, and then scale the result back. More about the Qm.n format can be found at `http://en.wikipedia.org/wiki/Q_(number_format)`. The only difference is that the actual Q1.7 format requires 9 bits, where the first bit is used for the sign. But because pixel values are positive, we can drop the sign bit and pack the Q1.7 format into 8 bits of a single byte.

In the following code, we demonstrate the use of the fixed-point arithmetic:

```
uchar src = 111;
float multiplier = 0.76934;
uchar dst = 0;

dst = uchar(src * multiplier);
printf("dst floating-point = %d\n", dst);

uchar fpMultiplier = uchar((multiplier * 128.f) + 0.5f);
dst = (src * fpMultipiler) >> 7; // 128 = 2^7
printf("dst fixed-point = %d\n", dst);
```

The following is the console output for that code. You can see that approximation is not exact, but again, we can tolerate it in our application. We can also try to use the Qm.n format with a larger value of `n`, for example, `Q1.15`:

```
dst floating-point = 85
dst fixed-point = 84
```

It can bee seen that fixed-point arithmetic uses integer operations instead of floating-point, and so is much more efficient. At the same time, it can be effectively vectorized with NEON, producing even higher speedups.

Please note that you shouldn't expect speedup in our example, as the NEON version is already good enough. But if the numerical pipeline is a little bit more complicated, fixed-point may give you an impressive speedup.

Detecting facial features (Advanced)

Many **human-computer interaction** (**HCI**) applications require knowledge about position of a face and facial features in a frame. We will learn how OpenCV can be used for detecting facial features. Detected faces are decorated in a way, as shown in the following screenshot:

Getting ready

The source code for this recipe is available in the `Recipe15_DetectingFacialFeatures` folder in the code bundle that accompanies this book. You can't use Simulator, as we're going to use camera in this recipe.

How to do it...

The following are the steps required to implement the application for this recipe:

1. Add a new C++ class to our CvEffects library, called FaceAnimator, together with its resources.

2. Implement the facial feature detection functionality.

3. Add some animation, based on the position of detected facial features.

4. Call this class from the video processing application.

Let's implement the described steps:

1. First of all, add a new class with the following interface to the CvEffects static library project. You should also add three XML-files with cascade classifiers (lbpcascade_frontalface.xml, haarcascade_mcs_eyepair_big.xml, and haarcascade_mcs_mouth.xml), and two images that are going to be used for animation (glasses.png and mustache.png):

```cpp
class FaceAnimator
{
public:
    struct Parameters
    {
        cv::Mat glasses;
        cv::Mat mustache;
        cv::CascadeClassifier faceCascade;
        cv::CascadeClassifier eyesCascade;
        cv::CascadeClassifier mouthCascade;
    };

    FaceAnimator(Parameters params);
    virtual ~FaceAnimator() {};

    void detectAndAnimateFaces(cv::Mat& frame);

protected:
    Parameters parameters_;
    cv::Mat maskOrig_;
    cv::Mat maskMust_;
    cv::Mat grayFrame_;

    void putImage(cv::Mat& frame, const cv::Mat& image,
                  const cv::Mat& alpha, cv::Rect face,
                  cv::Rect facialFeature, float shift);
    void PreprocessToGray(cv::Mat& frame);
```

```
        // Members needed for optimization with Accelerate Framework
        void PreprocessToGray_optimized(cv::Mat& frame);
        cv::Mat accBuffer1_;
        cv::Mat accBuffer2_;
};
```

2. Next, we need to implement the class's methods. In the following code snippet, we show the only the most important detectAndAnimateFaces method:

```
static bool FaceSizeComparer(const Rect& r1, const Rect& r2)
{
    return r1.area() > r2.area();
}
void FaceAnimator::detectAndAnimateFaces(cv::Mat& frame)
{
    TS(Preprocessing);
    //PreprocessToGray(frame);
    PreprocessToGray_optimized(frame);
    TE(Preprocessing);

    // Detect faces
    TS(DetectFaces);
    std::vector<Rect> faces;
    parameters_.faceCascade.detectMultiScale(grayFrame_, faces,
1.1,
                                             2, 0, Size(100,
100));
    TE(DetectFaces);
    printf("Detected %lu faces\n", faces.size());

    // Sort faces by size in descending order
    sort(faces.begin(), faces.end(), FaceSizeComparer);

    for ( size_t i = 0; i < faces.size(); i++ )
    {
        Mat faceROI = grayFrame_( faces[i] );

        std::vector<Rect> facialFeature;
        if (i % 2 == 0)
        {
            // Detect eyes
            Point origin(0, faces[i].height/4);
            Mat eyesArea = faceROI(Rect(origin,
                      Size(faces[i].width, faces[i].height/4)));
```

```
                TS(DetectEyes);
                parameters_.eyesCascade.detectMultiScale(eyesArea,
                    facialFeature, 1.1, 2, CV_HAAR_FIND_BIGGEST_
OBJECT,
                    Size(faces[i].width * 0.55, faces[i].height *
0.13)));
                TE(DetectEyes);

                if (facialFeature.size())
                {
                    TS(DrawGlasses);
                    putImage(frame, parameters_.glasses, maskOrig_,
                        faces[i], facialFeature[0] + origin,
-0.1f);
                    TE(DrawGlasses);
                }
            }
            else
            {
                // Detect mouth
                Point origin(0, faces[i].height/2);
                Mat mouthArea = faceROI(Rect(origin,
                    Size(faces[i].width, faces[i].height/2)));

                parameters_.mouthCascade.detectMultiScale(
                    mouthArea, facialFeature, 1.1, 2,
                    CV_HAAR_FIND_BIGGEST_OBJECT,
                    Size(faces[i].width * 0.2, faces[i].height * 0.13)
);

                if (facialFeature.size())
                {
                    putImage(frame, parameters_.mustache, maskMust_,
                        faces[i], facialFeature[0] + origin,
0.3f);
                }
            }
        }
    }
}
```

3. Now its time to use the `FaceAnimator` class in our application. First of all, set up the copying of the `FaceAnimator.hpp` public header file, so our application will be able to see the class. Then you should rebuild the library project. After that, you should add references to cascade files and images from the `CvEffects` project, as we did earlier.

4. Now, `FaceAnimator` can be used from the Objective-C code, as we did for the `RetroFilter` class in the *Applying effects to live video (Intermediate)* recipe. The following is the declaration of our `ViewController` class.

```
@interface ViewController : UIViewController<CvVideoCameraDelega
te>
{
    CvVideoCamera* videoCamera;
    BOOL isCapturing;

    FaceAnimator::Parameters parameters;
    cv::Ptr<FaceAnimator> faceAnimator;
}
```

5. We also need to load all the resources in the `viewDidLoad` method, then create a class instance in the `startCaptureButtonPressed` method, and apply processing in the `processImage` method. We don't show these methods, but they are almost identical to what we've written before for the `RetroFilter` class. You can build and run the application when all of the integration code is added.

How it works...

Let's consider how the `detectAndAnimateFaces` method works. You can see that the processing time of every step is measured, as the overall processing is quite expensive.

We are already familiar with detecting objects (and faces in particular) using OpenCV's `CascadeClassifier` class. You can see that we use a different cascade in this example, which is based on LBP-features (Local Binary Patterns). This cascade works several times faster than the Haar-based cascade and the quality doesn't differ much. And this performance difference is important, because we're going to process live video.

When the detection is completed, we sort the vector of detected faces by their size using the `FaceSizeComparer` function. The `for` loop is used to detect facial features within every face. We decided to detect eyes in every even face, and mouth in every odd face.

We use a couple of tricks to improve the quality and minimize the detection time. First of all, we limit the search area, so that eyes are detected on the upper half of the face rectangle, and the mouth in the lower half. This not only improves the performance, but also allows avoiding false detections. Secondly, we search only for the largest object using the CV_HAAR_FIND_BIGGEST_OBJECT flag. It stops the detection when the first object is found, so we don't waste our time searching for another pair of eyes or mouth in the same face rectangle. It is obvious that even if we find something, this should be a false detection. Finally, we control the minimal facial feature size. The following are empirically found minimal relative sizes for eyes and mouth:

```
Size(faces[i].width * 0.55, faces[i].height * 0.13) //eyes
Size(faces[i].width * 0.20, faces[i].height * 0.13) //mouth
```

Finally, we put some animation over the detected facial feature, using the alpha blending function from the previous recipes.

There's more...

This sample presents the very basic approach to facial feature detection. It can be significantly improved in both quality and speed. Let's consider some opportunities.

Performance

First of all, we need to detect performance bottlenecks and try to avoid them or optimize with NEON. In our example, it can be found that a `cvtColor` function takes a significant percentage of the processing time. It is a good candidate to be vectorized. Another candidate is alpha blending in the `putImage` function.

Tracking between detections

Another approach to optimize the performance is to run face and facial feature detection every *k* frames, and to run optical tracking between them. One can try to use the `calcOpticalFlowPyrLK` function on the points returned by the `goodFeaturesToTrack` method. If the `goodFeaturesToTrack` method also takes much time, we can cover the face rectangle with a simple regular grid of points. The median motion vector (after some filtering) can give us a hint about the new face position. **Median-Flow tracker** can be a good candidate for this task (`http://bit.ly/3848_MedianFlowTracker`).

Active Shape Model

One of limitations of the Cascade Classifier approach is that it returns only a bounding box, while some applications may need contour representation of a facial feature. There are some approaches that allow fitting a contour model of the entire face to an image. One of the most popular methods is **Active Shape Model** (**ASM**); several open-source implementations are also available.

There are also some other approaches; one of them was developed by Jason Saragih and is covered in detail in the book *Mastering OpenCV with Practical Computer Vision Projects*, *Packt Publishing*. The source code is available online at `http://bit.ly/3848_FaceTracking`.

Using the Accelerate framework (Advanced)

The **Accelerate** framework can be very useful for performance optimization, especially if your application intensively does some vector and matrix math, or signal and image processing. We will learn how to link the framework and process OpenCV matrices with it.

Getting ready

All the source code changes will be localized in the CvEffects library, so you can use the same Recipe15_DetectingFacialFeatures project. Again, you can't use Simulator, as we're going to use the camera.

How to do it...

In the previous recipe, we have profiled the FaceAnimator class and slightly improved the facial feature detection time by tuning the parameters. But the very first preprocessing step was still quite expensive, and we're going to optimize it using the Accelerate framework. In fact, we could work on a custom NEON optimization as before, but Accelerate could be a good time saver, as it provides a wide set of optimized functions for image processing. We will replace cv::cvtColor and cv::equalizeHist with calls to Accelerate functions. Histogram equalization helps the detection algorithm to better tolerate illumination changes.

The following are the steps required to accomplish the task:

1. Link the Accelerate framework to the project.

2. Declare two new functions: cvtColor_Accelerate and equalizeHist_Accelerate.

3. Implement them using the Accelerate API.

4. Replace the original FaceAnimator::PreprocessToGray method with the new FaceAnimator::PreprocessToGray_optimized method that addresses calls to the optimized functions.

Let's implement the described steps:

1. So, first of all, we need to link the Accelerate framework by navigating to **Build Phases | Link Binary With Libraries** in the project settings.

2. Then we will add these declarations to the Processing.hpp header file:

```
// Accelerate-optimized functions
int cvtColor_Accelerate(const cv::Mat& src, cv::Mat& dst,
                        cv::Mat buff1, cv::Mat buff2);

int equalizeHist_Accelerate(const cv::Mat& src, cv::Mat& dst);
```

3. Next, let's add a new Processing_Accelerate.cpp file to the CvEffects project, and insert the following code in it:

```
#include <Accelerate/Accelerate.h>
#include <opencv2/core/core.hpp>

using namespace cv;
```

```
int cvtColor_Accelerate(const Mat& src, Mat& dst,
                        Mat buff1, Mat buff2)
{
    vImagePixelCount rows = static_cast<vImagePixelCount>(src.
rows);
    vImagePixelCount cols = static_cast<vImagePixelCount>(src.
cols);

    vImage_Buffer _src = { src.data, rows, cols, src.step };
    vImage_Buffer _dst = { dst.data, rows, cols, dst.step };
    vImage_Buffer _buff1 = { buff1.data, rows, cols, buff1.step };
    vImage_Buffer _buff2 = { buff2.data, rows, cols, buff2.step };

    const int16_t matrix[4 * 4] = {  77, 0, 0, 0,
                                    150, 0, 0, 0,
                                     29, 0, 0, 0,
                                      0, 0, 0, 0 };
    int32_t divisor = 256;

    vImage_Error err;
    err = vImageMatrixMultiply_ARGB8888(&_src, &_buff1,
                                        matrix, divisor,
                                        NULL, NULL, 0 );

    err = vImageConvert_ARGB8888toPlanar8(&_buff1, &_dst,
                                          &_buff2, &_buff2,
                                          &_buff2, 0);
    return err;
}

int equalizeHist_Accelerate(const Mat& src, Mat& dst)
{
    vImagePixelCount rows = static_cast<vImagePixelCount>(src.
rows);
    vImagePixelCount cols = static_cast<vImagePixelCount>(src.
cols);

    vImage_Buffer _src = { src.data, rows, cols, src.step };
    vImage_Buffer _dst = { dst.data, rows, cols, dst.step };

    vImage_Error err;
    err = vImageEqualization_Planar8( &_src, &_dst, 0 );

    return err;
}
```

4. Now, we have to call this code from the `FaceAnimator` class. For that, add the members `accbuffer1` and `accBuffer2` of the `cv::Mat` type to the class' declaration, and add the following method to the implementation file:

```
void FaceAnimator::PreprocessToGray_optimized(Mat& frame)
{
    grayFrame_.create(frame.size(), CV_8UC1);
    accBuffer1_.create(frame.size(), frame.type());
    accBuffer2_.create(frame.size(), CV_8UC1);

    cvtColor_Accelerate(frame, grayFrame_, accBuffer1_,
accBuffer2_);
    equalizeHist_Accelerate(grayFrame_, grayFrame_);
}
```

5. Finally, use it instead of the original method, as shown in the following code snippet:

```
void FaceAnimator::detectAndAnimateFaces(Mat& frame)
{
    TS(Preprocessing);
    //PreprocessToGray(frame);
    PreprocessToGray_optimized(frame);
    TE(Preprocessing);

    ...
```

6. Build and run the application; you should see that the working time for the preprocessing step has shortened at least twice.

How it works...

First of all, you should see that Accelerate uses the `vImage_Buffer` structure as an image container. This structure is quite simple, but more importantly, it can be created on top of the existing OpenCV matrix. We don't have to copy or convert data, and that allows to seamlessly interleave calls to OpenCV and Accelerate, without any performance penalty. The following is how we initialize `vImage_Buffer` using `cv::Mat` data:

```
vImagePixelCount rows = static_cast<vImagePixelCount>(src.rows);
vImagePixelCount cols = static_cast<vImagePixelCount>(src.cols);
vImage_Buffer _src = { src.data, rows, cols, src.step };
```

Unfortunately, Accelerate doesn't provide color space conversions, and we have to use the generic `vImageMatrixMultiply_ARGB8888` transformation function. So, `cvtColor_Accelerate` is implemented in two steps, we first convert the RGBA input matrix to another four-channel matrix, first channel of which is the required grayscale image. Then we split the resulting matrix into four planes, and later use only the first one.

It should be noted that `vImageMatrixMultiply_ARGB8888` actually uses fixed-point arithmetic, and the numbers in the `matrix` variable are RGBA to Gray conversion coefficients, multiplied by 256. That's why we use 256 to initialize the `divisor`:

$Y = 0.299R + 0.587G + 0.114B \approx (77R + 150G + 29B) / 256$

After the conversion, we use `vImageConvert_ARGB8888toPlanar8` to get the first channel with the image intensity data.

Implementation of the `equalizeHist_Accelerate` is much more straightforward. We simply call the `vImageEqualization_Planar8` function, and use its result directly.

As a final note, the Accelerate framework (in contrast to OpenCV) wants the user to allocate all the input and output buffers manually, and of course to deallocate this memory later. That's why we call the `Mat::create` method for three image buffers in the `PreprocessToGray_optimized` method. You shouldn't be afraid of slow memory reallocations on every frame, as OpenCV doesn't recreate matrices if they are already in the desired format.

There's more...

We used only three functions from the Accelerate framework, but there are many more of them. Please refer to the official documentation if you want to know more: `http://bit.ly/3848_Accelerate`. You will see that many primitives from OpenCV's `core` and `imgproc` modules can be found there. Despite the fact that Accelerate's syntax is somewhat noisy, the use of this framework could be a cheaper solution, than to manually optimize every function with NEON. You should also note that Accelerate not only tries to exploit CPU (with NEON extensions), but also **Digital Signal Processor** (**DSP**), so it could provide a better speedup than a manually vectorized code.

Building OpenCV for iOS from sources (Advanced)

Sometimes, you may want to change the OpenCV itself, for example, to add some new cool feature, or to fix a bug. OpenCV's BSD-like license allows you to modify the library, and we'll learn how one can build a custom version of OpenCV.

Getting ready

There is no source code for this recipe, as we're going to build OpenCV. You will need a Git command-line client, CMake (Version 2.8.11 or higher), and Python 2.7 installed. Usually, Python is already installed on Mac OS, but the CMake tool needs to be downloaded from `http://cmake.org`. And, you don't need an iOS device, because the compilation is done on a host computer (so-called cross-compilation).

How to do it...

The following are the steps required to get your custom OpenCV build:

1. Create a new directory and clone OpenCV's source code repository there.
2. Check out the proper Git branch or tag.
3. Create a symbolic link to Xcode.
4. Run the Python script to build the iOS framework.
5. Update your project(s) to link to a new framework.
6. Modify the OpenCV code and rebuild the framework if needed.

Let's implement the described steps:

1. Almost all operations in this recipe should be executed on the Terminal. So, create a new Terminal window and create a new working directory for our experiments:

   ```
   $ mkdir ~/<working_directory>
   $ cd <working_directory>
   ```

2. Then we need to clone OpenCV sources, and we'll use the GitHub repository for that:

   ```
   $ git clone https://github.com/Itseez/opencv.git
   ```

3. When complete, we have to check out the branch or tag, which we're going to use as a starting point. Let's imagine we want to build the latest state of the 2.4 branch, which is used for the OpenCV 2.4.x releases' preparation:

   ```
   $ cd opencv
   $ git checkout 2.4
   ```

4. Now, let's create a symbolic link to Xcode, so the build script can see the compiler, header files, and so on:

   ```
   $ cd /
   $ sudo ln -s /Applications/Xcode.app/Contents/Developer Developer
   ```

5. We're now ready to build the framework. Please be patient, because it will take a while. OpenCV is going to be built in three different configurations, and it may take a couple of minutes:

   ```
   $ cd ~/<working_directory>
   $ python opencv/platforms/ios/build_framework.py build_ios
   ```

6. After the process is complete, your framework will be available at `~/<my_working_directory>/build_ios/opencv2.framework`. You can now add this framework to your Xcode projects, as we did before. When rebuilt, your projects will use this new version of OpenCV.

7. If you want to change something in OpenCV, you can edit its code and rerun the script. If that is possible, unchanged binaries from the previous build will be used, and the compilation will be faster than it was the first time.

How it works...

As we mentioned before, iOS frameworks are a better way to distribute your static libraries. In its core, they are simple libraries and headers, but they may contain binary code for several architectures (such as `armv7`, `armv7s`, and `i386` in our example). That makes them more convenient to link from Xcode projects, because you need not think about linker configuration, rather, you can simply add a reference to the framework.

So, the only interesting moment in this recipe is how the `build_framework.py` script constructs the OpenCV framework. You can actually study its source code to get complete understanding. For every architecture (old and new iOS devices, plus Simulator), it generates an Xcode project using CMake and executes Xcode in order to build it. When all three configurations are built, script forms the `~/<my_working_directory>/build_ios/opencv2.framework` directory properly, so it becomes a valid iOS framework.

When the script finishes its work, you can use the built framework as a normal OpenCV distribution.

There's more...

Despite the fact that it is quite easy to create your custom version of OpenCV, we encourage you to use the official one. The library is always in active development; new versions are rolled out regularly, so if you don't want to waste too much time merging your changes, better to stick to the official distribution.

All new source code should be developed outside of the library itself, as we did with the `CvEffects` project. And, if your development grows into something stable and useful, you can always contribute your code as a new OpenCV module, or as an extension to the existing one.

In case you've found a bug, you can live with your custom build for some time. But you should submit a GitHub pull request with the fix, so it is integrated into the development branches as soon as possible. The same rule applies to performance optimizations. If your code is faster, but still generic enough (you have tested it on multiple platforms and with different parameters), you can submit a pull request. This way we will have an even more stable and efficient library!

More information on the contribution process is available on the official website at `http://opencv.org/contribute.html`.

About Packt Publishing

Packt, pronounced 'packed', published its first book "*Mastering phpMyAdmin for Effective MySQL Management*" in April 2004 and subsequently continued to specialize in publishing highly focused books on specific technologies and solutions.

Our books and publications share the experiences of your fellow IT professionals in adapting and customizing today's systems, applications, and frameworks. Our solution based books give you the knowledge and power to customize the software and technologies you're using to get the job done. Packt books are more specific and less general than the IT books you have seen in the past. Our unique business model allows us to bring you more focused information, giving you more of what you need to know, and less of what you don't.

Packt is a modern, yet unique publishing company, which focuses on producing quality, cutting-edge books for communities of developers, administrators, and newbies alike. For more information, please visit our website: www.packtpub.com.

Writing for Packt

We welcome all inquiries from people who are interested in authoring. Book proposals should be sent to author@packtpub.com. If your book idea is still at an early stage and you would like to discuss it first before writing a formal book proposal, contact us; one of our commissioning editors will get in touch with you.

We're not just looking for published authors; if you have strong technical skills but no writing experience, our experienced editors can help you develop a writing career, or simply get some additional reward for your expertise.

Mastering OpenCV with Practical Computer Vision Projects

Step-by-step tutorials to solve common real-world computer vision problems for desktop or mobile, from augmented reality and number plate recognition to face recognition and 3D head tracking

Mastering OpenCV with Practical Computer Vision Projects

ISBN: 978-1-84951-782-9   Paperback: 340 pages

Step-by-step tutorials to solve common real-world computer vision problems for desktop or mobile, from augmented reality and number plate recognition to face recognition and 3D head tracking

1. Allows anyone with basic OpenCV experience to rapidly obtain skills in many computer vision topics, for research or commercial use

2. Each chapter is a separate project covering a computer vision problem, written by a professional with proven experience on that topic

3. All projects include a step-by-step tutorial and full source-code, using the C++ interface of OpenCV

Mastering openFrameworks: Creative Coding Demystified

A practical guide to creating audio-visual interactive projects with low-level data processing using openFrameworks

Mastering openFrameworks: Creative Coding Demystified

ISBN: 978-1-84951-804-8   Paperback: 358 pages

A practical guide to creating audio-visiual interactive projects with low-level data processing using openFrameworks

1. Create cutting edge audio-visual interactive projects, interactive installations, and sound art projects with ease

2. Unleash the power of low-level data processing methods using C++ and shaders

3. Make use of the next generation technologies and techniques in your projects involving OpenCV, Microsoft Kinect, and so on

Please check **www.PacktPub.com** for information on our titles

OpenCV Computer Vision Application Programming Cookbook

ISBN: 978-1-78216-148-6   Paperback: 350 pages

Over 50 recipes to help you build computer vision applications in C++ using the OpenCV library

1. Master OpenCV, the open source library of the computer vision community

2. Master fundamental concepts in computer vision and image processing

3. Learn the important classes and functions of OpenCV with complete working examples applied on real images

Instant OpenCV Starter

ISBN: 978-1-78216-881-2   Paperback: 56 pages

Get started with OpenCV using practical, hands-on projects

1. Learn something new in an Instant! A short, fast, focused guide delivering immediate results

2. Step by step installation of OpenCV in Windows and Linux

3. Examples and code based on real-life implementation of OpenCV to help the reader understand the importance of this technology

Please check **www.PacktPub.com** for information on our titles

www.ingramcontent.com/pod-product-compliance
Lightning Source LLC
Chambersburg PA
CBHW060202060326
40690CB00018B/4215